IRENE JONES

Irene Jones was a teacher at St. Gregory's School, Marnhull, who settled in Stalbridge. Once retired, she became absorbed in the history of Stalbridge and entered for the Mansell-Pleydell Essay Competition, a long-standing competition for original research into an aspect of Dorset history. Her essay entitled 'The Stalbridge Estate 1780–1854' won first prize in 1993, so she set about organising its publication as a paperback book entitled *The Stalbridge Inheritance 1780-1854*, still available today. At the same time she continued systematically gathering material for the whole of Stalbridge's history from its beginnings as a self-sufficient settlement.

In all this Irene Jones's situation was bitterly poignant. She had been diagnosed with cancer in 1988, at first considered treatable but by 1993 clearly terminal. We are particularly fortunate that through her determination she completed the manuscript of this present book for publication in the last weeks before her death on 25th September, 1993.

Now sixteen years later, the Dovecote Press is delighted to be able to publish this work which might otherwise not have seen the light of day.

At the wish of Irene Jones's son Richard, all the proceeds of this book are being donated to the Friends of St. Mary's Church, a charity established to preserve the fabric of Stalbridge Parish Church.

Following page
Stalbridge Market Cross,
engraved by Basire for the first edition of
John Hutchins *History and Antiquities of Dorset*, 1774.
(see pages 40-43)

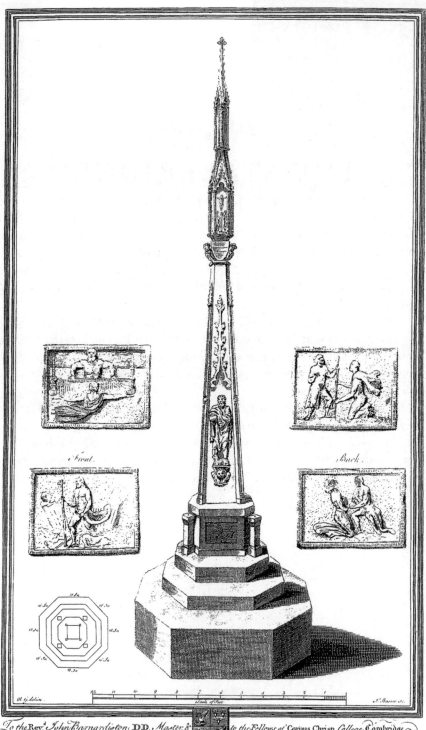

Front.   Back.

To the Rev.ᵈ John Barnardiston, D.D. Master &c. to the Fellows of Corpus Christi College, Cambridge.
This PLATE Engraved at their Expence is GRATEFULLY inscribed by the Author.

THE STALBRIDGE INHERITANCE

From Roman times to the late Eighteenth Century

IRENE JONES

THE DOVECOTE PRESS

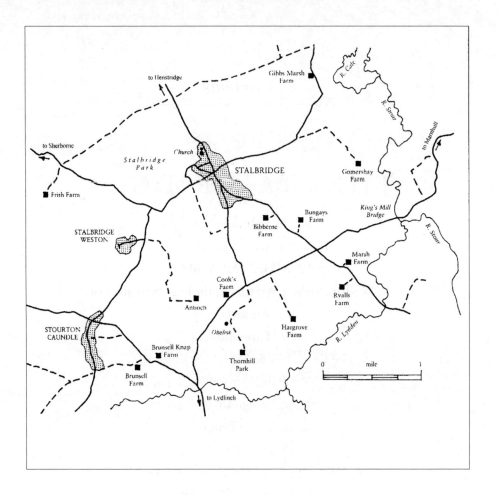

First published in 2009 by The Dovecote Press Ltd
Stanbridge, Wimborne Minster, Dorset BH21 4JD

ISBN 978-1-904-34971-6

Typeset in Sabon and printed and bound by KHL, Singapore
Printed on Munken 80 gsm paper.
All papers used by The Dovecote Press are natural recyclable
products made from wood grown in sustainable, well-managed forests.

A CIP catalogue record for this book is available
from the British Library

Contents

Foreword

This book comprises the first part of the history of Stalbridge, a work that was undertaken by Irene Jones in the early part of the 1990's following the completion of *The Stalbridge Inheritance* 1780-1854. This last named volume preceded it partly because sources of information were more readily available and perhaps also because peoples' interest was greater about more recent times.

However, there can be no story or history without a beginning and this volume of the history looks back through the available records to discover the beginnings of Stalbridge, its development as a self sufficient settlement, its struggles and achievements set in the context of the wider world and indeed the profound consequences of social, political, religious and military developments in the outside world upon the lives of the people of Stalbridge.

Now, 15 years later, publication of this section of the Stalbridge story has come about thanks to the enthusiasm, encouragement and energy of some of today's inhabitants of this settlement in Dorset that over the centuries has survived both success and misfortune and which today, still stands steadfastly on the splendid escarpment overlooking the Blackmore Vale.

Introduction

Stalbridge is first mentioned in Saxon Charters, and may have had a population of over one hundred inhabitants by the time of the Domesday Returns in 1087.

By 1285, the Abbot of Sherborne was granted a market in Stalbridge and the status of a market town was retained until the end of the nineteenth century; the population increased steadily until at the end of the eighteenth century, it was 1245 in 1801.

One of Stalbridge's main features is the fine late fifteenth century Cross, still standing in its original position, built, no doubt, at the centre of a large space which once held the market. Another is the five mile length of wall which surrounds Stalbridge Park, brought into Dorset literature by William Barnes, the Dorset Poet born in 1801 at Bagber, just south of Stalbridge, who wrote of '. . . Stalbridge wi' its grey-wall'd park . . .' in his dialect poem, *The Window fream'd wi' Stwone*.

Thomas Hardy, a reader of Hutchins' *History and Antiquities of Dorset* and with a keen ear for local lore placed the setting of his story, 'Squire Petrick's Lady', one of the *Group of Noble Dames*, in Stapleford (Stalbridge) Park, during the period when the magnificent Stalbridge House stood in the Park.

Stalbridge House, engraved for the first edition of Hutchins (see plate section), saw a succession of residents, some famous like the great Earl of Cork, and his son, Robert Boyle, the eminent scientist with an international reputation; some infamous like Mervyn, second Earl of Castlehaven, the first builder of the fine edifice, who was beheaded following a trial for 'unnatural practices' in 1631; and one Peter Walter, notorious for his money dealings and characterised by Henry Fielding in his novel *Joseph Andrews*.

The last owner of the mansion, the first Marquess of Anglesey, who survived a leg amputation at the Battle of Waterloo, having no personal interest in residing in the property, once visited by King George III and his family, allowed the 'goodlie faire house' to be ignominiously taken down. So disappeared from the Stalbridge landscape a house which had once ranked fifth largest in Dorset.

This volume of Stalbridge history deals with the early history of the small market town of Stalbridge until the end of the eighteenth century, when it belonged almost exclusively to the Earl of Uxbridge.

The HUNDRED of BRUNSELL
(Brunsella, Brownshall, Broneshull)

Situated in the Hundred of Brunsella, Stalbridge and Weston were given separate descriptions in the Domesday Book, but Weston never developed as a separate entity with its own church, although it had its own manor and was held by the Weston family for several centuries.

Eventually Weston was absorbed as one of the four tithings of Stalbridge together with Gomersay and Thornhill, the other being the Town Tithing.

The raised mound known as Brunsell's Knap on the Stalbridge/Stourton Caundle boundary was the focus and meeting place for the early consultations of the chiefs and owners of property in the Hundred, an area drawn up for the collection of taxes and other monies to the King.

The Hundred of Brunsell contained 52½ hides, and also included Stourton Caundle, Caundle Wake, Purse Caundle, Bishop's Caundle, Lydlinch Baret, and Stoke Gaylard.

VARIATIONS ON THE NAME

The name Stalbridge is derived from a bridge on staples or poles - stapul, post, pillar; pile or bridge built on piles. It has had many forms . . .

Stapulbreicge	998	Saxon Charter - Codex diplomaticus oevi Saxonici
Staplebrige	1086	Domesday Returns
Stapelbridge	1191	Will
Stapelbrugg	1243	Will
Stapelbrigg	1302	Lay Subsidy Roll Edw I
Stalbrigge	1327	Lay Subsidy Roll
Stalbriggh	1346	Feudal Aids
Stalbruge	1350	Extent of the Manor
Stappelbrigge	1351	Parson Robert de Braford in old deed
Stapelbrigg	1411	Lay Subsidy Roll
Stapleford	1530s	Leland
Stalbryge	1539	Tudor Muster Roll
Stawbridge	1569	Tudor Muster Roll

Weston survived intact, occasionally spelt Westone.

Gomershay offered variously, becoming Gomershaye 1327, Gommersheye 1332, Gomersby 1350, Gomerssaye 1539, Gomersey 1569, and Gomershay 1662-4, Gummershay 1902.

The commonly used spelling of Gomershay has been used throughout except where documents specify otherwise.

Thornhill likewise had variants which show the versatility of English phonetics and their interpretation viz. Thornhulle 1327, Thornhull 1332, Thornehyll 1569, Thornell 1598, Thornehill 1677.

ONE

Early Occupation

Of the few indications of early occupation of the Stalbridge area, it is not surprising that most of them were found on the higher ground above the flood plain of the River Stour and River Cale. The site chosen by the earliest settlers in Stalbridge must have been a desirable spot, well supplied with springs, woods and pasture and above any likely flooding. There is, however, no evidence of any large settlement in Stalbridge's past until the medieval period.

The two Roman villas at Hinton St. Mary and Fifehead Neville and the possibility of a settlement at West Stour suggest spasmodic development by the Romans in the Blackmore Vale area.

The finding of a sepulchral urn and quern by men digging for gravel in a field named 'Gomershay', near the River Stour around 1860/1870, raises questions about the location as a possible settlement because of its closeness to a river which easily floods and has caused well-documented problems over the last two hundred years. Unless the presence of many more trees, when Stalbridge was well-wooded and a part of the Forest of Blackmore, on the edge of the Forest of Gillingham, greatly affected the water-table, and hence the flood capacity, one can expect that the flooding occurred in Roman times.

A slight elevation of land, however, at King's Mill, protects the house and Mill from flooding, and this is the case across the river on the Stalbridge bank, where the twentieth century 'Golden Meadow' bungalow, although not far distant from the river, stands above the regular level of floodwaters.

When the sepulchral urn was unearthed

'Inside four slabs of stone a sepulchral urn was found, and with the urn a great number of Roman coins, more than a thousand in all, at least three hundred of which were in excellent preservation. There was also found at the same place a Roman quern, or hand mill.'

These coins were mainly of the age of Constantine, a similar period to coins found on Barrow Hill.

Two Roman coins, one bronze, one of copper, were also reported to have been dug up in Mr Lionel Parsons' garden in Gold Street. The copper coin, with a 'very perfect female head' on the obverse bore the inscription, LVCILLA AVGVSTA.

Occupation debris, indicating Romano-British settlement, was found on the slopes of Barrow Hill.

Further evidence of Romano-British occupation was discovered in April

1918, when excavations were taking place in the garden of Mr G. Prideaux in order to enlarge the buildings for the Creamery in Gold Street. A skeleton was discovered, lying facing East about 3 ft. from the surface, believed to be that of a male 6 ft. in height, with a small coin in its mouth. The bronze coin was much defaced, but AUG could be deciphered. It was stated in *Somerset & Dorset Notes & Queries* that the bones were deposited in the Dorset County Museum.

SAXON

In 705, when the area known as Dorset, the name being taken from Dornsaete or Dorsaeta, 'men of Dorchester', was held by the West Saxons, Sherborne had become established as the seat of a Bishop. The term Dorsetshire was not recorded in documents until about 940.

Situated between the two great Saxon Abbeys of Sherborne and Shaftesbury, Stalbridge appears to have aroused no developing interest in Saxon times except to be named in two Saxon Charters, when land was given by the King to the Church or Abbey of Sherborne.

860 x 866 Ethelbert, King of the West Saxons, to the church of Sherborne 20 hides at Stalbridge.

998 Ethelred, King of all Albion, to Wulfsige, bishop of Sherborne at the instance of Archbishop Aelfric . . . confirmation to the monks of their title to . . . 20 (cassati) in Stapulbreicge . . .

DOMESDAY

By the time of the Domesday Returns, Stalbridge was part of the Bishop of Salisbury's Sherborne estates. Weston, which belonged to the same Bishop, was given a separate entry. There is no mention of Gomershay or Thornhill, the Thornhill described in the Domesday Book referring to Thornhill, belonging to Wulfric, one of the King's Thanes, in the Hundred of Candenone, in the Wimborne area.

As a hide of land might have been 48 acres or 120 acres, it can be seen that Domesday Stalbridge occupied between a fifth and slightly less than half of the later parish. Stalbridge would then have been one of the outlying territories of Sherborne Abbey, on the edge of the Forest of Gillingham, almost on the boundary of the area around Sturminster, which belonged to the Abbey of Glastonbury. The well-watered countryside provided fat stock for winter meat, and there would be venison and game, and timber for fuel from the extensive woods to support the monks of Sherborne.

The Domesday Return for Stalbridge was as follows:

'The same bishop holds Staplebrige . . . in King Edward's time it paid geld for 20 hides. There is land for 16 ploughs. Of this 6 hides are in demesne, and there are 2 ploughs, with 1 slave; and 19 villans and 2 bordars with 11 ploughs. There is a mill rendering 15s and 25 acres of meadow, pasture, 4 furlongs and 2 furlongs wide, [and] woodland 1 league long and 3 furlongs wide. It is worth £12.

Of the same land Lambert holds 2 hides, and there he has 1 plough, with 6 bordars. It is worth 20s.

Of the same land also Manasses holds 3 virgates, which William the King's son took from the church without the consent of the bishop and the monks. There is 1 plough.'

Stalbridge has the distinction of giving the one and only reference in Sherborne Domesday Returns to any of William the Conqueror's sons, William Rufus, later William II. Why the King's son would want to acquire 3 virgates of land, which could have been as little as 90 acres, leaves much room for conjecture, unless it was mainly for hunting.

The number of people mentioned apart from Lambert and Manasses, who was a cook, were 19 villeins, 8 bordars and 1 slave; if men with an average of five per family, this would have meant a population of 140. The villeins, bordars and slaves were all bound to give service to the lord of the manor, working on his demesne land, but apart from the slaves, the lowest rank, with varying degrees of tenure.

An exact description of 11th century Stalbridge cannot be determined from the record because of the varying implications of each phrase; 16 ploughs, for instance, might have been pulled by two oxen each, or up to as many as eight, each team capable of ploughing an acre per day in season. It would be necessary to keep enough young bullocks to replace the older draught animals and also cows from which to breed and supply milk. The winter feed had to be sufficient to supply the teams and the stock not killed off for meat and salting.

The requirements for each ox, cow or horse would be one acre for summer grazing and one acre of hay for supplementary winter feeding. Sheep and goats would also require one acre each for summer grazing. The staple diet of the inhabitants would have been bread, meat and wild fruits, and ale or mead to drink.

Weston, now included in the parish of Stalbridge, in Domesday belonged to the same Bishop of Salisbury, and in King Edward's time had paid geld for 6 hides.

'There is land for 6 ploughs. Of this 5 hides are in demesne, and there are 2 ploughs, with 1 slave; and 7 villans and 7 bordars with 3 ploughs. There are 12 acres of meadow, [and] scrubland 4 furlongs long and 1 furlong wide. It is worth £7.'

Smaller than Stalbridge, Weston must have a moderately sized hamlet at this time with a possible 75 inhabitants.

By 1086, therefore, the area of land that later became the parish of Stalbridge had two separate centres of occupation, surrounded by their open fields: the rest of the area was "waste" or common covered with forest or pasture.

TWO

Early Medieval Period

DISPUTES

Early medieval legal disputes reveal the settlement of certain parts of Stalbridge, although the case brought by William, son of Robert Tenent, in 1213/14 against his father's former wife, Maria, concerning 1/3rd part of a virgate of land states merely that the land was in Stalbridge, for which William gave Maria 20s.

Even the Abbot of Sherborne, to whom most of Stalbridge belonged, was involved in a dispute at Schyreburn (Sherborne) in 1243/44 with John Enrys, chaplain, over one virgate of land in Stapelbrug, which was to belong to John and then revert to the Abbot. It is not stated where John held office.

The name of John de Antioch appears in a dispute in 1266/67 with Henry de Haddon over one messuage and one carucate (hide) of land in Stapelbrigg, for which Henry gave John 40 marcs of silver.

Forty years later, in 1308/9, Henry de Haddon and Alianora, his wife, were involved in a dispute with Thomas de Marleberge of the manor of Caundel Haddon (later Stourton Caundle), when the messuage and carucate of land in dispute was deemed to be Henry's. Henry and Alianore, his wife, were involved in a further case brought against Thomas de Marleberge in 1334. (Thomas de Marleberge was Sheriff of Dorset several times during the reign of Edward II, 1307-1327.)

Other disputes concerned one messuage and land in Nywenham (Newnham), 1315/16, and three messauges, one carucate and 75 acres of land in Gomershay, Newnham and Stalbridge in 1327.

DEVELOPMENT

Any developments in Stalbridge during this period would have taken place under the authority of the Abbot of Sherborne.

There must have been a substantial church in Stalbridge, if one looks at the fourteenth century arcades of the nave which have survived in St. Mary's Church and the vestiges of north and south transepts. Possibly there was a sprinkling of dwellings around the church, with rights on common land, which was later enclosed in 1618 by the Earl of Castlehaven to the great annoyance of the inhabitants.

From the medieval details still to be seen in the dwelling in the High Street known as Silk Hay, believed to have been a substantial merchant's house, it is likely that medieval Stalbridge had already encroached down the hill from the church and that houses lined the one great street as in Leland's description of the 1530s.

The fact that a market charter was granted to the Abbot of Sherborne for Stalbridge in 1286 and a further charter for a market and fair in 1335 would confirm the growth of the village and the need for a money-based economy, instead of barter. There would be rents to be gained from tolls and the prospect of financial gains. The early markets were no doubt held in the space where the Cross was built in the late fifteenth century.

Between the twelfth and fourteenth centuries, new settlements at the edge, or beyond, the open fields of Stalbridge were recorded at Frith Farm (1244), Antioch (1244), Newnam (1244), Thornhill (1244), Hargrove Farm (1285), Gummershay Farm (1315), and Marsh Farm (1327). All were ring fence farms and all the farm names, except Newnam (later Ryall's) survive today.

It is likely that Gibbs Marsh Farm, Bungays Farm, Bibburne Bridge Farm and Cook's Farm date from the same period.

LAY SUBSIDY ROLLS

During the early years of the reign of Edward III (1327-1377), in order to finance payment to deal with trouble in Ireland and Scotland, Parliament granted to the King the money collected from taxes assessed on the Lay Subsidy Rolls of 1327 and 1332.

Details of the 1332 Lay Subsidy Roll are given here, with some reference to the Roll of 1327. From the Lay Subsidy Roll of 1332, the four tithings of Stalbridge in the Hundred of Brunsell were assessed separately, and the numbers of those assessed, were Stalbridge 34, Weston 18, Thornhill 10, and Gomershay 10 names.

The two chief taxers for Dorset for this Roll, and also for the 1327 Lay Subsidy Roll, were John Peuerel and Roger le Guldene, with sub-taxers appointed to assess and record the value of movable goods on Michaelmas Day last. Household goods, tools and foodstuffs of the peasant, artisan and farmer were not included in rural areas. The rest of the goods, which were assessed at one fifteenth, would include the value of the yield of crops, peas, beans, grain, hay and honey, as well as horses, cattle, sheep, pigs and goats.

1332 LAY SUBSIDY ROLL

In Stalbridge, Johanne de Hamme paid 6s, Philippo atte Bergh 3s, Johanne Wymel, Roberto le Chipman, and Adam atte Hole each 2s.

The other 29 people paying 18d or less were:-

Adam Capon	Willelmo Eustaz	Thoma Purchaz
Willelmo Sharpe	Dauid le Gulden	Johanne Persons

Ricardo atte Mulle	Thoma le Smyth	Waltero Goudgrom
Thoma le Haiward	Roberto le Sarmoner	Johanne Maynard
Editha Wryngge	Willelmo Reympel	Johanne Paltyn
Ricardo le Bouchere	Johanne atte Bergh	Johanne Rodel
Waltero Beau	Ricardo le Maister	Johanne Bonnard
Henrico le Reue	Willelmo Osmond	Petro Pyc
Dauid atte Welle	Hugone Berlegh	Johanne Poschers
Henrico Oschou	Johanne Aubyn	

(The main differences in payments between the 1327 and the 1332 Lay Subsidy Rolls are that Johnne de Hamme's assessment increased from 4s 6d, Philippo atte Bergh's from 2s, and Adam atte Hole's from 6d. Beatrice atte Brigge (12d) disappeared altogether.) (Note. Did David le Gulden give his name to Gold (Gould) Street, and did Editha Wryngge then live at the place called the Ring, when it was perhaps circular?)

There were 18 taxpayers in Weston with Johanne Radgar paying 3s:
Johanne le Calewe, Johanne le Noble, Edwardo atte Hole, Waltero atte Nassh, Roberto atte Frythe, Thoma atte Brouke, and Thoma atte Thorne each paid 2s. The rest paying 20d or less were:

Roberto atte Broke	Johanne Niwman	Roberto Morman
Willelmo Shenyng	Henrico le Freynssh	Waltero le Kyng
Willelmo Laurencz	Johanne Pleystret	Henrico atte Hile
Roberto le Hopere		

(In 1327, Johanne Radgar paid only 2s and Johanne le Noble 3s.)

In Thornhill, Johanne de Thornhulle paid 4s, Hugone de Cokkul 2s.4d, Waltero de Thornhull 20d, Henrico Quarry 20d and paying less than 18d were:

Johanne le Veym	Galfrido le Gaunt	Johanne de Haregraue
Dauid le Bole	Johanne le Gengger	Johanne Le Boster

(In 1327, Johanne de Thornhulle paid 3s.)

At Gommeresheye, Agnete de Percy paid 4s, Johanne de Lillyngton 3s, Editha atte Thorne paid 2s.4d, while Johanne Chedhorn, Ricardo de Pusele, and Cristina de Pusele each paid 2s. the rest paying 19d or less:-

Johanne Richeman	Johanne Rodel
Hugone Crey	Johanne Shireue

(Johanne de Percy assessed at 12d in 1327, disappeared from the 1332 Roll; a more descriptive name is given in 1327 to Johanne Rodeel, that of Johanne Rondel in la Mersch.)

Out of the four tithings, the scattering of more wealthy persons seems to be evenly balanced, with Stalbridge holding the greatest number by far of the lesser taxpayers.

Roberto de Stalbrigg in the 1332 Roll was assessed for xviijd at Stocke in Lydlinch. In 1327, however, his name appears in Stalbridge, assessed at 12d.

THE BLACK DEATH

From all we know of the impact of the Black Death, which entered England through Melcombe Regis in Dorset in August 1348, and reached London by November, it would be incredible to believe that Stalbridge could not have suffered losses in this terrible scourge.

It may be that the Manorial Extent of the Manor of Stalbridge, taken for the Abbot of Sherborne in 1350, reflects the anxiety of the Sherborne monks about the state of the labour force in the surrounding countryside. This must have been seriously depleted in some areas, and have had its effect on customary works when the villeins and serfs were in increasing demand and stating their own terms because of fewer numbers available.

The end of the Extent of the Manor gives a reminder of the death of the Abbot, himself probably a victim of the plague which is said to have wiped out almost half of the clergy in England, the pattern repeated in the area controlled by the Abbess of Shaftesbury, who was herself a victim, and where new vicars were appointed at Shaftesbury on 29 November, 10 December, 6th January and 12th May.

MANORIAL EXTENT OF THE LANDS OF
THE ABBOT OF SHERBORNE 1350

The simplicity of life in the fourteenth century derived from the descriptions of the three tithings, Stalbridge, Weston and Gomershay, for the Abbot of Sherborne, under whose ownership they were to continue for a further two centuries, is perhaps deceptive (Thornhill, the fourth tithing of Stalbridge, was not part of the Abbot's lands).

Parliament was continually being asked for money by the King to fund the wars with France, and thereby having to impose more tax charges.

The servile labour force in the country was becoming restless and asking for more for their work when they knew that hands were scarce. Commutation for labour services was already becoming established by the time of the Black Death, thus lessening the hold over physical labour on the lord's demesne.

The lack of labour due to the plague meant that crops could not in some places be harvested and prices of food rose. Landlords, including ecclesiastical owners like the Abbot of Sherborne, also felt the economic effects of the rise and fall of agricultural prices and the consequences of the lack of workers.

The Statute of Labourers in 1349 was an attempt to control the labourers by preventing them from leaving the parish or refusing work, and forbade the offering of wages higher than those of three years earlier. Butchers, bakers and fishmongers were also restricted to some fixed prices.

The Survey of the Manor of Stalbridge in 1350 may have been a direct result of the Black Death. The result is purely an economic assessment. There is no count of the number of people left after a national catastrophe, nor is there any valuation on housing apart from the capital messuages.

In the 1350 Extent of the Manor, one almost senses the peacefulness of the rural scene, but the reality was harsher, as in Langland's *Piers Plowman*, who wrote of the lot of the poor and the poor man's wife 'suffren muche hunger,/ And wo in winter-tyme'.

Details of the Extent of the Manor of Stalbruge were taken on the Monday next after the Feast of Epiphany in the year 1350 (23 Edward III), and were given on oath before an Escheator, Thomas Cary, by Walter Tylye, John Baldewyn, John Bromstel, John atte Woodland, John Russel, Nicholas le Clerk and others (not named).

There is there one capital messuage which is worth nothing per annum above reprises. And one garden of which the fruit is worth 12d per annum, and herbage . . . 12d. And one dove-cot which is worth 40d per annum. And 310 acres of arable land . . . worth 102s 6d per annum, price 3d per acre. And 26 acre of meadow which after mowing are in common and are worth 26s, price 12d per acre. And winter pasture there from the feast of St Michael to the feast of Easter is worth 13s 4d. And summer pasture there from the said feast of Easter to the feast of St Michael is worth 26s 8d. And pleas and perquisites of the Court are worth 20s per annum. And from the rents of free tenants there 70s 8d to be paid at the terms of the feast of St Michael, the Lord's Nativity, Easter, and the birth of St John the Baptist in Equal portions. And from the rents of customary (tenants) there 106s 8d per annum to be paid at the same terms of the year in equal portions. And works of the customary (tenants) there from the feast of St Michael to Lammas Day (1 August) are worth 11s 6d. And certain carriage works called Slatlode at the feast of St Michael are worth 4s 4d. And owed from Cherchesshutte at the feast of St Martin 26 hens . . . worth 3s 3d, price 1½d per head. And that the same Abbot (of Sherborne) died on 17 December next before.
Sum £19 10s 3d.

It can be seen that the pattern of life was one based on religious festivals, where the worshippers at Church could not fail to know when their rents were due, nor, if they were not free tenants, could they afford to ignore reminders of their customary work due to the Abbot, that is the amount of labour due to him, according to status.

Apart from Easter, a moveable feast, the other dates are fixed: Birth of St John the Baptist, 24 June; Lammas Day 1 Aug.; St Michael, 29 Sept.; St Martin, 11 November. The rents were paid quarterly by the free tenants at Easter,

Midsummer, Michaelmas and Christmas.

From the one large house, there was nothing to be made above the rent-charge, but the dovecote in Stalbridge was worth just 1d more than the 26 hens owed by the church. It is interesting to note that the arable lands were quite extensive at 310 acres for a traditionally wet area, but there is no price given for grain, nor is ploughing mentioned, although it may have been included in the works of the customary tenants. The 'certain carriage works called Slatlode' are hard to define exactly, but taking place at Michaelmas they could mean the cartage of wood for repairs or firing, or re-building materials.

The Oaths for Weston were made by William de Weston, John Jouste, Walter Payn, William Lauren, Jordan Chyld and others, not mentioned.

'There is one capital messuage worth nothing per annum beyond reprises.
. . . a certain close worth 40d per annum.
. . . 104 acres of arable land worth 45s per annum, price 3d an acre.
. . . 12 acres of meadow worth 12s per annum, price 12d per acre.
. . . winter pasture, Michaelmas to Easter, worth 3s 4d.
. . . summer pasture, Easter to Michaelmas, worth 10s per annum.
. . . from assize rents, 42s 6d to be paid (quarterly) in equal portions.
. . . customary works from Michaelmas to Lammas Day, worth 9s 8d.
And owed from Chercheshutte at the feast of St Martin 13 hens, worth 18½d (sic), price 1½d per head.
. . . pleas and requisites of the Court there, worth 5s per annum.
Sum £6 12s 2½d.

The Extent of the manor of Gomersby (Gomershay) follows the same pattern as the above; it was sworn on the oaths of John Hook, William Warman, William Lovel, Walter Coffin, Richard atte Wodehouse, William Kirkeby and others that there was

'. . . one capital messuage which is worth nothing above reprises, but there is there one garden the fruit of which is worth 12d per annum.
And herbage 18d. And 120 acres of arable land, worth 30s 3d per annum price 3d an acre.
And 11 acres of pasture . . . worth 22s per annum.
And winter pasture from the feast of St Michael to Easter . . . worth 2s.
And summer pasture from the same feast of Easter to St Michael . . . worth 6s.
And from rents of assize there 6s 7d to be paid at the Baptist in equal portions.
And that the same Abbott died on the said 17 December.
Sum 58s 4d.

The value of the manor of Gomersby was small compared even with Weston and it must be noted that no customary tenants paid rents and no customary works were due. Was it a case of the men having been wiped out by the plague?

Gomersby, however, did have a garden worth as much as that of Stalbridge.

No garden is given for Weston and only Stalbridge had a dovecote. All the free tenants appear to have been in Stalbridge.

Other Acts to control labour were passed in 1360, when the letter 'F' (for fugitive) could be branded on the head of a labourer, caught after fleeing his parish, and in 1363, when certain men engaged in husbandry had to wear only blanket or russet cloth.

The labouring population was depleted by further outbreaks of the plague, which occurred in 1361 and 1369. In the latter half of the century, the restlessness of rural communities, aggravated following the imposition of the Poll Tax, finally led to the Peasants Revolt in 1381. It is not known whether Stalbridge inhabitants were involved, nor is there any indication of the numbers who suffered in the several visitations of the plague.

THREE

Weston, Callew Weston, Stalbridge Weston

Having its own entry in Domesday quite distinct from Stalbridge, Weston surprisingly did not develop as a separate village with its own church. Like its larger neighbour, Stalbridge, it belonged to the Abbot of Sherborne from whom the Westons leased land, the value in 1293 being £7.2s.6d.

In 1313, William de Weston was called as a juror at an Inquisition of the Forest of Gillingham, whereby it was recorded that 'The family dwelled at Westesun in the paroche of Staplebridge, and yet do.'

The Lay Subsidy Rolls of 1327 and 1332 record Weston as a Tithing of Stalbridge.

CALLEW WESTON

According to information gathered from unpublished family documents in 1892, the Le Calews and the Westons of Callow Weston were the same family.

Dune's Weston in early deeds was also identified as Callow Weston, which was a separate manor, distinct from that of Stalbridge Weston.

In 1403, the manor of Cale Weston was in the possession of Hugh Weston and his wife, Amicia. By 1503, when another Hugh Weston was Lord of the Manor, the manor and lands were held of the Abbot of Sherborne at 6s 8d per year and the Lord of Tomer, who received as his due a pair of white gloves as chief rent.

A dispute of 1607 revealed that

' . . . the plott of common ground called the old waye was . . . almost adjoyninge to Mr. Weston's backside,' (i.e. at the back of his house), ' . . . Mr Weston's mansion house and demesnes of Calew Weston.'

Evidently this house was in a corner of Stalbridge great park, where the outlines of an E–shaped foundation could then be seen, and after Callew Weston was sold to Peter Walter, Lord of the Manor, tradition had it that the manor-house became a cottage in Stalbridge Park, retaining a fine Elizabethan chimney-piece as a relic of its former glory.

A story was told that upon the transfer of the property, Peter Walter entertained his neighbour, Mr Weston, to supper, whereupon next morning, Mr Weston found that in a state of intoxication the previous evening he had signed away his property for the sum of 1500 guineas. Although receiving the money from Peter Walter, Mr Thomas Weston hid it, in his bitterness at his folly, in a furze faggot stack at his home, Hargrove Farm, from where some of his men stole it and set the stack on fire to conceal the theft. The story is probably based on fact; the date of the property transaction cannot be verified, but the story suggests the 'smart' negotiations of the parsimonious Peter Walter, who was buried 29th January, 1745/6, and succeeded by his grandson, also called Peter Walter.

The application to enclose Stalbridge Park, and incorporate the Weston mansion house, was not made until three years after the death of Peter Walter, grandson, above mentioned, by his brother, Edward Walter, who enlarged Stalbridge Park and built the wall round it.

A map of 1760, showing the newly-enclosed and enlarged Stalbridge Park, contains a large area marked the 'Late Mr Weston's Farm', which would, no doubt, be part of Callew Weston mentioned above, and would explain why the foundations of Mr Weston's house were in the corner of the Park.

STALBRIDGE WESTON

The documents that came to light in 1892 quoted above state specifically that the manor of Stalbridge Weston was quite distinct from that of Callew Weston, and that until the Dissolution it was held by Sherborne Abbey after which it was disposed of by King Henry VIII to Watson and Twynnyhoo, who sold it to Richard Brook. It then descended to Duke Brook and Charles Brook of Templecombe. Christian Sprinte, daughter and co-heiress of Richard Brooke, at various times held a Court of the Manor.

In 1607, Duke Brook wished to declare the manor of Callew Weston as being dependent on the manor of Stalbridge Weston, subject to a yearly rent of 10s, but it was shown that the payment which had been made to Sherborne Abbey, was for that of the office of Almsgiver, (Pittansarye) and not for the manor, and the matter was refuted by Hugh Weston.

In 1611 Stalbridge Weston was granted to George Thornhill Esq, but in 1663 Edward Thornhill sold the manor of Stalbridge Weston to William Whitchurch, linen draper of Frome Selwood, Somerset. William Whitchurch was also acting as Court Baron of Stalbridge Weston Manor in the Manor Court held in 1665.

William Whitchurch, Esq., held a Court of the Manor of Stalbridge Weston in 1703. (In two documents of May 1662, William Whitchurch was listed as a linen draper of Frome Selwood, Somerset; in 1663, William Whitchurch was a grocer in the negotiations for the sale of the Manor of Weston.) By 1671, both William Whitchurch the elder, merchant of Frome Selwood, and William Whitchurch the younger (no occupation given) are mentioned in the same document for the assignment of the manor.

Robert Thornhill was obliged to sell Thornhill and all his lands in Stalbridge, which included those in Stalbridge Weston, in 1686 for £6,300 to Sir William Pysent of Urchfont, Wilts.

In 1696, Rymples, a tenement and land, (74 acres) was sold by William Weston for £630 to Elizabeth Pitt of Curry Rivel.

There followed in 1702 the sales of Hill House and land, Hargrove and Locketts by Sir William Pysent to the Westons in connection with the marriage of William Weston, junior, to Betty Brune, daughter of Charles Brune of Plumber, in the parish of Lydlinch.

Without confirmation, it is likely that the old deeds of the manor of Stalbridge Weston came into the hands of the Westons of Callew Weston at this time, but on a document of sale dated October 1733, Peter Walter was described as Lord of the manors of Stalbridge Weston and Anteox.

Following the death in 1763 of Thomas, son of William and Betty Weston, the last male heir, the division of the remaining Weston estates fell by lot in 1792 to Thomas's three sisters; Newnhams (Ryall's) to Betty, married to William Helyar of Coker Court; Hargrove and Locketts to Mrs Anne Greening, and Frith House and lands to Mary, wife of Richard Wright, M.D.

A mural monument in Stalbridge Church records the deaths of William Weston of Calewe Weston in 1727, aged 59, and his wife Betty, in 1765, aged 82. Their son, Thomas, died in 1763, aged 52 years, and was buried like his parents in the vault in the Weston Chapel, which was re-dedicated as the St. Joseph Chapel in 1969.

Certain documents reveal that Frythe House existed in the 17th century, although it was one of the medieval settlements around Stalbridge noted as early as 1244. Frith House was of consequence in the Manorial Court Rolls of Stalbridge Weston for 1666, when the inhabitants were demanding furze and wattle for house repairs from 'Freth' Wood and right of access through 'Freth' House and Grounds.

Thomas Weston Esq was fined by the same Court for not appearing to do his free suit and service, but it cannot be certain whether he lived in Callew Weston Manor House, which was absorbed during the next century by Stalbridge Park. It was not likely to be Frythe House because in 1659, Hugh Weston the younger, aged 29, was living there.

From a map of Stalbridge, drawn by a local man, Edward Curray, in 1738, both Hill House and Weston House are given locations, but Frith House is not. It is, however, likely that until Stalbridge Park was enclosed, the Westons were using the three houses as their homes, and for some periods, Hargrove also at Thornhill.

Fragmentary documentation shows that in 1702, William Weston took on a lease of Hill House for one year.

In 1744, Thomas Weston and his mother, Betty Weston, widow of William Weston signed a lease and release of Frith Farm to Charles Brune of Plumber. By 1800, the properties had left the Weston heirs and were owned by William Fryer of Frith Farm.

The Rental Accounts paid in 1784 to Lord Paget, who inherited the estates of Peter Walter, contain the names of Lifehold Tenants in Stalbridge Weston.

Those holding Tenements and farms or land were:

Robert Drake	1 Tenement & 38 acres
John Hobbs	1 Tenement & 66 acres
Ann Lewis	2 Tenements & 3 acres
Samuel Shepherd	2 Tenements & 24 acres

Tenements only:-

Thomas Bazeley	Martha Deacon	Wm Hain
Wm Piner	James Snook	Anthony Snook
Lawrence Tulk	Robert Williams	Joseph Williams

Land only (in acres)

Joseph Apsey 62a	Thomas Burge 28a	Thomas Davidge 28a
Rev Davis 16a	James Dowden 49a	Mary Kember 43a
Thos Lanning 44a	Harry Lemon 18a	John Lewis 34a
John Loader 35a	Thos Mundane 47a	Thos Shepherd 22a
Widow Snook 5a	Silas Tizzard 11a	Edith Williams 22a
Thos Williams 4a		

The separate returns to Parliament of 1811 show that the tything of Weston contained 35 houses, inhabited by 37 families, with a total of 173 people.

FOUR

Antioch

Lying under the hill on which stands Thornhill Spire, along a lane branching off the north side of the road from Stalbridge to Lydlinch Common, is the ancient manor of Antioch, once the seat of the Antioch family. John de Antioch granted lands to William Thornhull by charter, unfortunately without date.

The name of Antioch has long been a matter of conjecture as to whether the place took its name from a Crusader, or whether it had any connection with Tarent Antioch, one of the early settlements amongst the Tarrants, south of Blandford.

John of Antioch appears to have been a landowner in 1266/67, when Henry de Haddon brought a case against him, regarding one messauge and a carucate (possibly between 60 and 180 acres) of land in Stalbridge, which Henry de Haddon retained, giving John de Antioch forty marcs of silver.

The name of Nichi de Antioch appears in a Lay Subsidy Roll of 1302/3. The thirteenth century dating of the name, Antioch, makes the suggestion of a Crusader's connection a possibility, more so if one links it with Galfridus de Mervin of 1309, and the stories attached to the later Stalbridge Cross. One must add here the fact that the Knights Templars had a station in Templecombe and a command garrison at Ansty, near Tisbury.

The strange carving on stone contained in a medieval Stalbridge house could also be linked to the Crusaders.

By 1385, when part of the land at Antioch, like much of Stalbridge, belonged to the Abbot of Sherborne, the remaining part of the estate had already passed from the first owners, the Antiochs, to the Haddons, (the lords of the manor of Caundle Haddon, later Stourton Caundle), who called it Haddon Antioch, and from them to the Fitzwarrens. Ivo Fitzwarren, the owner in 1385, was required to do homage to Abbot Goude of Sherborne, for the lands held of him in Antioch in the parish of Stalbridge.

When John Chidiock, Knight, died in 1450, he held 240 acres of land in Antioch and Caundle Marsh of Alianor, Countess of Arundel, and also 287 acres of land in Antioch and Caundle Marsh of William, Abbot of Sherborne.

By the time Leland visited Stalbridge, it had been in the possession of several families.

'Antioch dwellyd, or had lande in Staple Bridge paroche; and there is Antioch wood. His landes cam to Chidioke, and from hym onto Great Arundel, of

Cornwall; and the Stourtons lordes by partition.'

Antioch appears to have had the same owners as the neighbouring parish of Stourton Caundle. From the Stourtons, it was sold in 1700 to one William Whitchurch Esq. of Frome Selwood, possibly the son of the William Whitchurch who negotiated the sale of the manor of Stalbridge Weston in 1662. In the Assignment of the Manor of Anteox in 1701, further members of the family were included, namely, Edward Whitchurch, clothier, and Jonathan Whitchurch, mercer, both of Frome Selwood. It is evident that the family of Whitchurch continued to ply their trades in Frome, whilst putting money into owning lands in Stalbridge.

The family appears to have been descended from Samuel Whitchurch, mercer, who died in 1658 and of whom, William, first mentioned in Stalbridge documents in 1662, was one of seven sons. Nearly one hundred years later, in 1741 and 1742, Frome, 'that once wealthy cloathing Town' was suffering from a decline in trade and 'Decrease of the Woollen Manufacture'.

The Antioch Estate eventually passed to the Walter family, and then to Lord Paget, later Earl of Uxbridge.

On the Stalbridge Estate Rental Roll of 1784, Robert Drake was a Lifehold tenant of one tenement and 2 acres in Anteox. He also rented land in Stalbridge Weston.

The other lifehold tenants of land in Anteox in 1784 were:

James Banger	26 acres	James Robins	27 acres
Wm Snook	11 acres	Tite & Dober	10 acres
John Tulk	68 acres	Samuel White	100 acres

FIVE

Thornhill

Thornhill, lying two miles to the south-west of St. Mary's Church, became one of the tithings of Stalbridge.

Lands in Thornhill were granted by John Thornhull in 1227 to Ralph, his brother, and in 1274, John de Antioch granted lands in Stalbridge to Walter de Thornhull and in 1293, Margaret de Hargrave granted Hargrave to Walter de Thornhull. In 1337, John le Veyne released all his rights in his lands of Hargrave to another Walter de Thornhull. However, only Johane de Thornhull is mentioned in the Lay Subsidy Rolls of 1327 and 1332. In 1391, John Thornhull de Hargrove held six virgates of land in Thornhill of the Abbot of Sherborne, paying yearly one farthing.

The Thornhills maintained their family seat in Thornhill and Leland in the 1530s recorded that in a chapel of St. Mary's Church

'there one Thornehull of Thornehull lyeth buried on the South syde of the quir, in a fayre chapell of his owne building . . . '

Leland travelled

'From Stapleford onto Thornhul, a myle by good grounde enclosed. Here dwellith Master Thornhul an auncient gentleman. From Stourminster over the bridge and less than a mile further, I passed over a bridge of four arches that standeth as I remember over Devlles broke, and thens aboute a mile onto Thornehull. Thornehul dwelled at Thornehill in Staplebridge, and yet doth.'

Hutchins stated that the principal place of residence of this family was Thornhill and their 'place of sepulture in the south aisle of the church in Stalbridge belonging to them'.

In the Patent Roll of 31 Henry VIII, the Manor of Woolland was granted to William Thornhull of Thornhull, after which date there seems to have been a gradual move towards keeping Woolland as the main residence.

Several Wills of the Thornhulls, however, include the wish of the testator to be buried in the church at Stalbridge and William (died 1557) left 2s to the Common Box there and to 'eight poore men, each a gown of black'.

During his lifetime, William donated 66s 8d to making and mending the Shaftesbury to Sherborne Causeway; an order made in 1554 placed the onus of repairs on the parish through which the highway passed, William may have owned land near the highway or was generous in his donation as one of the travellers along it. He left to Johane, sheep, 20 kine, 1 bull, 8 oxen and a wain, and amongst his belongings were 2 silk beds, 8 feather beds, 20 prs sheets, 8 prs blankets and 8 coverlets.

Robert, whose Will was proved in 1574, willed his body to be buried in the parish church of Stalbridge 'or in some other place in which it shall happen me to decease', leaving 6s 8d to the church and 6s 8d to the poor of Stalbridge. He left demesne lands at Thornhill and lands also in Bagber, Southfields, Woolland, Alweston, Russell, as well as the parsonage of Stourpaine, mentioning also 'all other household implements, including four feather beds, now being at Woolland'.

Thomas Thornhull, whose Will was proved in 1611 left 10s to Stalbridge Church and 6s 8d to Lydlinch. He gave his house of Hargrove and other properties to his father, William (also died 1611), and Barbara, his mother.

Their son, George, married Margaret Hull of Tolpuddle, and became grandfather of Sir James Thornhill, the famous painter, who restored the lands of Thornhill to the family following the mortgaging and selling of parts of the estate during the seventeenth century.

The manor and farms of Thornhill and Stalbridge Weston had been settled on George Thornhull for life in a family settlement dated 21 April 1648, but after George's death in 1656, Edward his brother raised mortgages on Thornhill in 1657. Although the Thornhull family, including George, father, and two sons, George and Edward, signed the Protestation forms for Woolland in 1641/2, the Hearth Tax Return for Thornhill, 1662/4, shows Edward Thornhull as the owner of Thornhill House with its fifteen chimneys, making it the second largest dwelling after Stalbridge House.

Stalbridge Weston manor and lordship were sold by Edward Thornhull for £3,000 in 1662; Edward died in 1676 and his son, Robert sought further mortgages on Thornhill from Butler Buggins in 1686 on terms for 86 years.

The sale by Robert of the capital messuage, farm and demesne lands of Thornhill to Sir William Pynsent for £6,300 in 1686, meant the breaking of family connections in Thornhill that had existed for centuries, the Thornhull family retaining the seat at Woolland, several miles from Stalbridge under the shade of the northern slopes of Bulbarrow.

It was left to the most famous of the family, the painter, Sir James, using the spelling, Thornhill, who was knighted by George I, to buy back the family possessions and rebuild Thornhill House to his own design, and add the obelisk in 1727.

SIR JAMES THORNHILL

James, the third son of Walter Thornhull, was born in Melcombe Regis in 1675 in the house called The White Hart in Lower Bond Street. The Melcombe Regis Parish Register clearly shows the name of James Thornhill, baptized 7th September 1675.

His father, listed as a grocer in Dorchester, married Mary Sydenham in 1668.

James had two older brothers, but the eldest, Samuel, was buried in 1681. Because of a debt, the boys' father left home soon after James was born and is known to have travelled abroad to America and Ireland.

Walter owed money to his sister-in-law, Francis Sydenham, wife of his cousin, Robert Thornhull of Woolland and absconded, but was later involved in a Chancery suit in 1691, which revealed part of his erratic life.

It seems likely that he had other secrets, one of which has only just come to light. In 1697 at the meeting of the Dorset Quarter Sessions, an application was made for an order for 18d per week to be paid to Piddletrenthide Overseers of the Poor for a male child, son of Walter Thornhull of Woolland, Gent., so that he would not become chargeable on the parish. It appears that for several years past he had been kept with the parish and 18d per week was ordered for 'so long time as the said child shall continue at Piddletrenthide'. As there was only one member of the Woolland family named Walter, one must draw conclusions, and feel sympathy for his neglected family in Weymouth.

The young James Thornhill in Melcombe Regis, great-grandson of Colonel William Sydenham, Governor of Weymouth in the early days of the Rebellion, and later Colonel-in-Chief of the Parliamentary Forces in the County, was obliged to seek a profession outside Dorset.

His great-uncle, Dr Thomas Sydenham, known as the 'English Hippocrates' for his accurate observations and recordings of the effects of diseases upon patients, well ahead of his time, lived in London, and it was under his guidance that the young James received tuition from Thomas Highmore, Serjeant-Painter to William III.

Thornhill was also able to travel abroad to Holland, Flanders and France, and some critics thought that he was influenced by the work of Verrio and Laguerre. It was against stiff competition from these and other foreign artists, the Pelligrinis and the Riccis, that Thornhill had to fight for his commissions.

The fashion in new building and gentlemen's houses at this time was decoration in the grand manner with large-scale murals and painted ceilings. For the work required in the Great Hall of the Greenwich Hospital, designed by Wren, now the Royal Naval College, Thornhill was engaged from the year 1708. One of the largest decorative schemes undertaken, Thornhill did not complete the painting until 1727.

Thornhill decorated several country houses, including Blenheim, Moor Park, Herts, Easton-Weston, Northants, Wimpole Chapel, near Cambridge, and he was also employed in copying the Raphael cartoons in the princesses' apartments at Hampton Court.

Altar pieces were painted at All Souls' and Queen's College Chapels, Oxford, and in Dorset, at St. Mary's Church, Melcombe Regis. Elsewhere in Dorset, his paintings exist in Charborough Park, and on the staircase of Sherborne House, once Lord Digby's School for Girls, in Sherborne.

A painting by Sir James of the Resurrection was given by Rev R. Frome, from the private chapel of Middlemarch Grange, to Folke Church.

ST PAUL'S CATHEDRAL

From 1675, the year in which Thornhill was born in Melcombe Regis, stone was being carried from the Portland Quarries in Dorset for the re-building of St Paul's Cathedral in London, burnt down in the Great Fire of London.

For this greatest of Wren's masterpieces, Thornhill was successful in being the artist chosen to paint the Dome, although the reasons why were not perhaps the most flattering to his personal vanity. Archbishop Tenison, one of the Trustees of the newly-completed building, being no judge of painting, had insisted 'first that the painter be a Protestant; and secondly that he be an Englishman'.

The commission nearly cost Thornhill his life. While he was stepping back to look at his painting under the Cupola, his foot almost touched the edge of the platform, and it was only the presence of mind of his assistant, who began to rub out his work to attract his attention, that saved Thornhill from falling off.

For this huge and somewhat hazardous undertaking, begun in September 1715, Thornhill was paid £2 per square yard. By 1719, he had finished the Cupola with illustrations from the life of the Apostle Paul in eight grisaille panels picked out in gold. Accounts of the Cathedral Library show that for painting and gilding of the Cupola, Lantern and Tambour (Whispering gallery), Thornhill received in 1721 a total of £19,375.

In recognition of his services, Thornhill was appointed Serjeant-Painter to King George I in 1720 and in the same year he became the first English painter to receive a knighthood.

Thornhill opened a drawing-school in his own house in Covent Garden after failing to interest Lord Halifax in a government-supported academy for artists. William Hogarth, later to become his son-in-law by marrying his daughter, Jane, was one of his pupils.

WEYMOUTH

From 1722, Sir James Thornhill represented Melcombe Regis in Parliament. For his native birthplace, he built almshouses; the memorial stone now in the Dorset County Museum, Dorchester, is inscribed Mar 30, MDCCXXII; he also deposited £2,000 as a fund for founding a hospital for Twelve Decayed mariners.

Through his friend, George Bubb Doddington, Thornhill was granted the Freedom of Weymouth in 1721, and he, in turn, presented a painting of the Royal Coat of Arms to the Guildhall. This is now retained in the Weymouth Museum together with a painting of Thornhill attributed to Hogarth.

SIR JAMES THORNHILL AND THORNHILL HOUSE

In 1720 there was a bargain and sale of the capital messuage and manor of Thornhill for £8,000 by the Pynsents, whose family had bought the property in 1686, and in the document of 10 April, 1721, the manor of Thornhill was to await the inheritance of Sir James Thornhill of St Paul's Covent Garden.

When Sir James acquired his family's ancestral estates at Thornhill, he rebuilt the house, possibly to his own design.

The East Elevation of the House, drawn for Isaac Sage's Thornhill Estate Map of 1775, shows a central bell and clock tower, but the tower had disappeared by the mid-nineteenth century.

The Thornhill bell, inscribed LAUS DEO I THORNHIL MDCCXXXI, now hangs in Milton Abbey School.

It is believed that until 1810, Thornhill's painting of the drawing room ceiling with his head in the centre was in good preservation, but it was later removed. The mantelpiece which he designed still remains.

William Barnes, the Dorset Poet, who could see Thornhill House on the horizon, not two miles distant from his boyhood home in Bagber, wrote to the *Gentleman's Magazine* in 1832 stating that it

> 'had originally a picture gallery or painting room extending its whole length (I believe about 100 ft) but as it occasioned a scarcity of habitable rooms the present owner of the property, W. Boucher Esq., has converted it into two splendid apartments.'

Swayne, writing in 1889, recorded the following story;

> 'There was formerly a beautiful ceiling in the drawing room, painted by Sir James Thornhill, with his head in the centre. This remained in good preservation till about 1810, when it was taken down by the tenant and carried away to preserve it from the wet, which came into all the other ceilings but it was afterwards brought back very much injured, and the house fell into a very ruinous condition.'

In 1727, Thornhill erected an Obelisk in the grounds in honour of the accession of George II. It was blown down in a great storm of 1836, but later reconstructed.

Sir James died in Weymouth in 1734, leaving a son, John, in favour of whom Sir James resigned the office of Serjeant-Painter in 1732.

John inherited the Thornhill Estate. His sister, Jane, was married to Hogarth, the painter. Sir James's wife, Judith, about whom little seems to have been discovered, not even her surname, lived until she was 84 and was buried in Twickenham.

Stalbridge Parish register records the burial of Sir James Thornhill on 10 May 1734. A pulpit was presented to the church soon after his death, for which the Churchwardens paid one shilling for the presentment and eleven shillings for 'riteing the pulpit and materials for same'. There is now no trace of the tomb, nor the 'fayre chapell' in which the Thornhills were buried.

In 1898, the present Exeter Pulpit replaced a two-decker one, no doubt the 1734 Pulpit, and the new Vestry added in 1876, now the Parish Room, was built over what may have been the site of the Thornhill Chapel on the south side of the choir.

High up in the East Window of the Parish Room is a vestige of stained glass wedged between the leads. This used to be the East Window of the Chancel, removed when the Powys Memorial East Window was inserted in the 1890s. It contains the Thornhill Coat of Arms, the chevron gules between three blackbirds. The arms of the Thornhill family are carved on the Chancel pillar next to the Table Tomb with blank shields under which it is believed that a Thornhill lies buried.

Tradition relates that there is a piece of his handiwork still surviving in Stalbridge Church. The unbearded head on the Evangelist pillar between the chancel and the Thornhill chapel is of different material and different style to the other three heads. It is said that the head was carved and placed there by Sir James Thornhill to replace one that had been destroyed and that he copied the features from those of his noble patron, George II.

Sir James's son, John, died in 1757, and it was his son, also John, who sold the Thornhill Estate in 1770 to Isaac Sage. It is from a map that he commissioned when he was in possession in 1775, that we know what Thornhill's design may have looked like before the house was altered again in the nineteenth century.

In the return to Parliament of 1811, a total of 191 people lived in Thornhill in 40 houses (41 families).

SIX

The Church of St Mary's, Stalbridge

The Church of St. Mary commands a prominent position on rising ground overlooking the valley of the River Stour. From many points from within the parish one finds oneself drawn upwards to the building, the substance of which has dominated the profile of Stalbridge for more than ten centuries.

Standing somewhat isolated on the outer fringe of present clusters of dwellings, it is likely that the medieval church was more at the centre of the developing town of Stalbridge until 1618, when fifty acres to the north and west of the church were enclosed as the Old Stalbridge Park and the rights of common taken away from the inhabitants by Mervyn, Earl of Castlehaven.

Vastly altered by restorations in the latter half of the nineteenth century, the church had before that date retained little of its medieval appearance. There is little evidence of the early church building.

The earliest record in the list of incumbents for the Church of St. Mary is that of Robert de Bradford in 1342, but the Saxon Charters in 800 and 998 give evidence of land in Stalbridge belonging to the Abbey of Sherborne.

Papal Bulls of 1145 and 1163 confirmed the possessions of the Abbot of Sherborne which included the church of Staplebridge, with all tithes and other appurtances, and the vills called Stapelbridge and Weston; an undated Charter of Henry II (1154-1189) granted to the sacristy of Sherborne, the church of Stalbridge for ever.

One might wonder why, in 1191, Stalbridge Church was exchanged like bartered goods, when William, Abbot of Schireburn, granted the churches of Lyme and Halgestok and the advowsons to the Bishop of Sarum, in return for the churches of Stapelbrige and Stokes.

It can not be certain, however, that John Enrys, named as Chaplain in a dispute with the Abbot of Schyreburn in 1243/4 over one virgate of land in Stapelbrug, held office in Stalbridge Church.

In 1285, John of Stapelbrigge was elected Abbot of Sherborne. It is significant that the first market charter for Stalbridge was granted soon after this date. The seal of John of Stapelbrigge, Abbot of Sherborne, was found in 1900, close to the old gate house of the Abbey at the east end of the churchyard. It was found at the time of the taking down of Mr Tuffin's shop, afterwards rebuilt.

The seal was the Abbot' personal, not his official seal, and was inscribed

S.JOHI'S D STAPELBRIGGE

Sigillum Johannis de Stapelbrigge

An early undated charter listed in the Calendar of Muniments at Sherborne

House, Gloucester, confirmed that William de la Wyle, Rector of the church of Stapelbrigg, gave to John Gerherd and his heirs, his rights to parts of Chilfrome. William must have been Rector of Stalbridge before 1342.

Within St. Mary's Church today, medieval building is retained only in the north and south arcades of the late fourteenth century nave, the capitals of the pillars having at some time been defaced and covered with plaster; and there are vestiges of north and south transepts from the same period.

The font, with greensand bowl and Ham Hill stem on a modern plinth, is early thirteenth century, older than any part of the existing church. A fourteenth century piscina can be seen in the east wall of the south transept.

The fourteenth century doorway and staircase, formerly leading to the rood loft, are in the south respond of the archway to St. Joseph's Chapel, and the old Sanctus bell turret still remains on the eastern gable of the Nave.

At the time of the Reformation, the church consisted of a chancel with a north chapel of the early sixteenth century, and, perhaps, a south chantry chapel and a broad rood screen separating it from a nave of four bays with north and south aisles and a south transept. The tower was somewhat squat.

Leland wrote of the south chapel:

> '. . . there was one Thornehull of Thornehull lyeth buried on the South syde of the quir, in a fayre chapell of his owne building . . .'

For some years, this was the principal burial place of the Thornhills, who had seats at Woolland and Thornhill; there is one visible remnant of the Thornhills now in the Parish Room; in the stained glass of the East window you can see the blackbirds on a thorn tree from the Thornhill coat of arms.

It is recorded that the first legible entry in the Parish Register was that of a Thornhill, dated 1540. Unfortunately, the Registers before 1691 appear to have been lost between the publication of the first edition of Hutchins and the third edition of 1869-1870.

CHURCH GOODS 1552

During the reign of Edward VI, inventories were made of Church Goods throughout the country and it is clear that before the 'surplus' items were taken from Stalbridge to end up in carts and wagons lined up before the buyers and smelters in London, the Church wore a much more colourful aspect. However, changes were taking place inside the churches, stone altars were replaced by wooden tables and a first *Book of Common Prayer* had been introduced and services conducted in English.

From the list reproduced on the following page, it is possible to gain an idea of some items of church furniture and usage; for instance, there appears to have been a main altar and also a side altar, and note the 'towell' for the 'fonte'.

First one pase of siluer gilte, ij chalis, one gilte, thether vngilte, one pixe of syluer parcell gilte, one payre of Crewetes of Syluer, ij Crosses of coper ij pair of Crewetes of Tynne iij paxes, one of whyte bone, another of Brasse, & another of coper, iij Sacrynge belles one sencer of Laten, iij payre of Stertes (handles?) pf Brasse, iij corporas, iij corporas clothes, V Cussyns of Sylke, One Suet of vestmentes of whyte Damaske with a cope to the same & an Aulter clothe of the same, one Suet of vestementes of grene Silke, with a cope, to the same, one payre of blacke Damaske, one payre of blewe Silke, one payre of whyte checker silke, one other payre of whyte Silke, one Cope of checked Silke, iij clothes for the Aulter, iij for the syde Aulter of diaper iiij frontes of stayned clothes a dexte clothe of the same, iij payre of cutrens stayned iij Towelles, twoo napkyns ij kerches for the Crosse, one fyne towell of diaper ij dexte clothes of diaper ij towelles for the aulter, one towell for the fonte, iij Syrples ij rochetes, iij Belles in the towre.

    To the churche use - Appoyncted by the said commyssioners one chalis vngilte one cope of grene Silke, with all the table clothes and Syrples The reste commytted to the charge of then vnder wryten

William Vowell curat		Hugh Weston	)	
William Kayleway	) churche-	Thomas Snoke	) parisheoners	
John Jenes	) wardens	Thomas Atwaters	)	
		John Jenes Junior	)	

The taking away of the 'superfluous' ornaments left very little for the use of the church in the form of one chalice and that the ungilt one.

During the same year, 1552, a second *Book of Common Prayer* was ordered and to add to the confusion of change, the reasons for which were probably not understood by the rural populace, unaware of the meaning of transubstantiation and the finer points of the Protestant movement that was sweeping across Europe, when Edward died the next year to be followed by the reign of Queen Mary, the images and other practices were re-introduced.

Once Mary had married her Spaniard, Philip, she brought back heresy laws and burning of Protestants, and it would be interesting to know how John Barnstable, the last Abbot of Sherborne who was Rector of Stalbridge from 1540-1560, dealt with the contentions during this period of radical and drastic measures, formalised eventually with the reign of Elizabeth.

The loss of Registers precludes information about the church during the Civil War, but from the Orders issued by the Dorset Standing Committee, it is obvious that there was some confusion in Stalbridge, if not defiant opposition.

In March 1647, John Savage was ordered to Stalbridge to receive all tithes and profits '. . . allowing the fifths unto Mrs Douch and her children according to the ordinances of Parliament'.

The Rector, William Douch, who tutored Robert Boyle, was 'outed, sequestered and silenced' for his 'delinquencie and scandall' before his death on June 11th, 1648, his son, William Douch, the younger, gent, having been ordered in April of that year to collect and gather the tithes of lands in his possession. During the same month it was stated that the churchwardens had not 'persued' an order to gather tithes, and 'Edward Dyer, clerke, cannot receive salary', and the Standing Committee once more ordered the churchwardens to gather tithes as directed together with Osmund Plant and Henry Townsend.

Later in 1648, John Devenish was ordered to Stalbridge to receive £150 per annum and to 'enjoy the parsonage house'. This meant that the Douch family had been driven from the Rectory, but it is not known whether the family received the fifths as ordered. Other 'intruders' who officiated in Stalbridge until the institution of John Douch were Nicholas Fairclough, died 1656, and Richard de Shute, ejected 1662.

For the first edition of the *History of Dorset* by Rev. John Hutchins, certain entries were copied from the first Register and John Douch is given as Rector of Stalbridge from 1652-1665. John Douch's signature as Rector is given on the document authorising John King, chosen by the parishioners of Stalbridge, to keep the register in 1653. Officially, he was re-instated as Rector in 1662, remaining in his position until he died in January, 1675/6.

It is believed that the pillars of the Weston Chapel (now the Chapel of St. Joseph) were spared defacement during this troubled period during the Civil War, as described below.

WESTON CHAPEL (now CHAPEL OF ST. JOSEPH)

Once the Weston Chapel, and now re-dedicated, the arms of the Thornhill family are on the easternmost pillar of the sixteenth century three bay arcade leading from the chancel.

The table tomb nearby with sides enclosing blank shields is from the late fifteenth or early sixteenth century and is a Thornhill tomb.

The other pillars with cherubims, evangelists, shields and scrolls resemble those in Holwell Church. The scrolls bearing, Latin inscriptions, were spared in the time of Cromwell because they had bible texts painted over, hiding the Latin. They have since been uncovered. The half pillar nearest the altar "Orate pro animnabus benefactorum". [Pray for the souls of the benefactors (of this church).] The figures on the second pillar are three of them bearded and one unbearded and represent the Evangelists.

"Sanctus Mattheus Evangelista.   Sanctus Marcus Evangelista.
Sanctus Lucas Evangelista.   Sanctus Johannes Evangelista."

Tradition suggests that the unbearded head, being of different material and different style from the other three heads, was carved by Sir James Thornhill as a replacement, the features copied from those of his patron, George the second.

The third pillar bears the inscription "Non Nobis Domine, non nobis sed nomine tuo da gloriam". [Not unto us O Lord, not unto us, but unto Thy name give the glory.] Until the Restoration of the Church in 1878 these sentences were painted over with English texts from the Gospels.

Against the north wall of the chapel, a life-size cadaver effigy lies on a table tomb of the late fifteenth or early sixteenth century, under which there is a Weston vault.

For three centuries, this chapel was known as the Weston Chapel, the Weston family holding land in Stalbridge Weston. Directly above the table tomb there is a seventeenth century wall monument to Thomas Weston, son of the Lord Chief Justice of Ireland, and Anne, his wife.

> In perpetvall memory of Thomas Weston of Calewe Weston Esq., and Anne his wife, son and heir to Sir William Weston, Knt., and Lord Chiefe Jvstice of Ireland.

Beneath are these lines called "The Avthor's Epitaph"

> I sawe my yovth was past,
> My age so fast crepte on,
> Not long my life covld last;
> Wherefore I thovght vpon
> This little tombe to make,
> My body for to rest,
> Desiring God to place my sovle
>
> In heaven amongst the blest.
> She that lies here and rests within this tomb,
> Had Rachel's face, and Leah's frvitfvl womb,
> Abigail's wisdom, Lydia's faithful heart,
> With Martha's care, and Mary's better part.

On the north wall of the chapel is the memorial in parallel columns to the Rev. W. Douch, chaplain to the Earl of Cork and tutor to Robert Boyle who lived with him as a boy. The translation reads

> Under this altar lies the body of the reverend and most learned William Douch, Rector of this Church, died June 11th in the year of his fate 1648, in the 70th year of his age. To me to die is gain. I shall arise. How long, O Lord?
> Feed my lambs.

> Here also lies the body of Joana Douch, his wife and a pious matron. Died October 4th, in the year of the Lord 1667, in the 84th year of her age. We die unto the Lord. And let the wives be subject to their husbands.

> They are good Catholics who follow the whole faith and a good life.

In the S.W. angle of the same chapel is the inscription;

> Anno Do. 1667
> Here lyeth the Body
> of Ciscily Freke, the

davghter of Thomas
Freke of Hinton, Esq.
who dyed December
the eight day.
Children
Remember yovr Crea-
tor in the Dayes
of yovr yovth
While the evil
Days come not.
Below;
Anno Dom. 1667
Here lyeth the
Body of Francis Freke who died
February first.
These two sisters
That were born to have
a nvptiall bed
have found a
nvptiall grave.

A large gravestone with its inscription in Lombardic capitals has been re-set and clamped to the south west wall of the chapel. At the restoration of the church it was transferred from the chancel, where William of Exeter, Rector of Stalbridge, lies buried, and let into the pavement behind the organ blower's seat, (then in the Chancel), much to the chagrin of the Rev. W.S. Swayne, who thought in 1889 that it would be too exposed there and effaced by wear. It was later moved to its present setting, where it can be seen and will not suffer from tread.

The stone, of Purbeck Marble, is thought to date from the thirteenth century, certainly not later than 1350, when Lombardic capitals went out of use and were superseded by the Black Letter character.

Swayne wrote 'the most modern known specimen of Lombardic capitals is on the tomb of Robert de Bures, Acton, the date of which is 1361.'

The translation around the tombstone, probably the earliest piece of work in the church, belonging to the 13th century, reads

Here lies in the tomb Master William of Exeter once rector of this church, to whose soul may God be propitious.

The chapel used to be filled with pews facing inwards to the chancel. A finely carved pew back with poppy heads was purchased and placed here in the nineteenth century. It now separates the choir from the chapel; the twelve panels are carved with emblems of the twelve apostles, the bag for Judas being by the west pillar.

THE EIGHTEENTH CENTURY CHURCH

Of St. Mary's Church in the eighteenth century, little is known of its interior, but from the Churchwarden's Accounts, it appears to have been necessary to build a 'new gallery for the singers' in the west end of the church in 1721 at a cost of £16; there were boxed pews, made of oak, and later, a two-decker pulpit. From the same accounts, it is evident that there was also an old gallery.

There is no record of the disappearance of the Thornhill Chapel, but it is possible that Sir James Thornhill was buried in it after his death in 1734. Having died in Weymouth, he was brought to Stalbridge and buried on the 10th May, presumably with his ancestors in the Chapel 'on the south syde' of the church. A pulpit was erected later in the year, undoubtedly to his memory.

By the time of the death of Peter Walter, Lord of the Manor of Stalbridge, a Vault had already been made 'in the Isle belonging to' his Mansion House in the Parish Church of Stalbridge, where he expressly wished 'to be buryed very privately'. He was buried on 29th January, 1745/6, and his grandson, Peter, was also buried in Stalbridge.

The Vault was still in existence after 1800 when, the Curate of Stalbridge, Rev. F.V. Luke, a descendant of the Walters, wished to have the vault opened in order to bury his little boy, and requested the Lord of the Manor, the Earl of Uxbridge, for permission to open the Vault for his burial.

The Lord of the Manor, if in residence, also occupied a special pew. Vouchers for work done in the late eighteenth and early nineteenth centuries show that regular repairs and maintenance were carried out on the special pew, the accounts being paid for by the estate.

Before the nineteenth century restorations, the boxed pews of oak, considerably more draught proof in what must have been a less-efficiently heated church, must have created a darker, heavier presence than that of the open pine seats of today.

The west gallery must have added to a gloomy aspect cutting out light from the church which was narrower before the extension of the north aisle in the nineteenth century alterations.

All traces of any refinements carried out for the Lord of the Manor on his special pew, which occasionally needed repairs, were removed when the box pews were replaced.

SEVEN

The Rectory

The advowson of the living of Stalbridge belonged to the Lord of the Manor until it was sold in 1697 by John Clements and Lord Viscount Shannon to Archbishop Tenison, who gave it to Corpus Christi College.

The appointment of the Rector, Rev Richard Wright, had been made in 1694, but soon after the advowson was in the hands of Corpus Christi College, a new Rectory was built in 1699, the lead rain-water head on the south side of the building still retaining the inscription, R.W. 1699.

Emblems of the arms of Corpus Christi, fleur-de-lis and pelicans, were placed on the newel-posts at the bottom of the flowing staircase in the Rectory.

The size of the Rectory, with its spacious ground floor rooms, several bedrooms and attics, created an imposing dwelling in a town of buildings of modest proportions, where, after Robert Boyle's Stalbridge House with its 30 chimneys (1 false returned), the next in size in the Hearth Tax Returns of 1662/4 belonged to John Douch, clerk, with 10 chimneys. Only 3 houses had between 5 and 10 and most in the Town Tithing had fewer than 4 chimneys.

One assumes the Church built the new Rectory on its own land near the Cross. The Abbot of Sherborne had at some time 'a maner place on the south side of the church'. If the 'maner place' had been on the site behind the huge wall at the back of the Rectory, this would help to explain the presence of a well-buttressed wall and the reason for its existence. As yet this can only be conjecture unless new evidence comes to light about the date of its construction.

There is also the possibility of a manor house on the south side of the church before Stalbridge House was built in 1618. There is no indication that the church owned the large house facing the church which was the Court House for the Manor and part of the Walter estate by 1780.

In 1795, dilapidations allowed for church property included a cottage on the 'Nap' which was thatched, Parsonage House and 'Vickarage House'.

We know from the description given by Robert Boyle, who was sent to live with his tutor, the Rev. William Douch, that the situation of the seventeenth century Rectory was not two musket shots away from Stalbridge House.

Although musket shots must carry variable distances, the weight of the later evidence suggests that Douch's old Rectory was not far from the newer one built next to the Cross.

From the Tithe Map of 1838, the Church still owned the land to the north of the Cross and Vicarage House, with one acre of land attached, was still in existence just opposite the Rectory on the other side of Duck Lane. This possibly could have been the house that Robert Boyle lived in with Mr Douch. In 1795, it was re-furbished, but when application was made to the Church Commissioners to take the house down in 1842 in order to use the stone for the building of Thornhill School, it was stated that the house had not been lived in for about forty years.

The re-furbishments in 1795 to Vicarage House are revealing. The name, however, remains a mystery when there presumably was never a Vicar of Stalbridge, unless the land at some time was subject to vicarial tithes.

In 1795, four chamber doors were replaced and a further four chamber doors on the ground floor. A new staircase was added with twelve feet of handrail and square banisters and a great deal of new elm flooring. There were new windows and a new window bench and boards. Outside a new end was placed on the 'Horse House Quarter', and a new rafter and wall and the thatch repaired on the Slaughter House. New doors, dunns and seat were given to the 'Necessary House.'

The total bill came to £35.12s.8d. which was a substantial amount, but slightly less than repairs to the 'Parsonage House, Barn and Brewhouse' which totalled £54.9s.6d., enough, however, to suggest that the house was worthy of preserving and rather more commodious and elaborate than the average cottage.

In the Parsonage House, as it was known for over a century, new floors were put in the garrets, a new hearth in the back garret, a slab of Marnhull stone in the Hall, and a new oak door in the wine cellar.

It was a most substantial house and garden for the Rector and servants, and in the Census of 1841 as many as twelve people were living in it. The site of Vicarage House was used for the building of the new school in 1873, the stone having been taken away to build the new school in Poolestown in the 1840s.

EIGHT

Stalbridge Cross

Standing in a prominent place by the side of the A357, Stalbridge Cross is a glorious reminder of past workmanship and prowess.

Because of the continual stream of heavy traffic passing through Stalbridge, there exists a continual hazard, far greater than those of the Civil War, storms, riotous crowds of the eighteenth century and bombs of the Second World War. In spite of its defaced carvings, worn away by time and weather, it can be said today, as much as it was in Pope's day, when he wrote his book, *The Old Stone Crosses of Dorset*, that it remains one of the finest crosses in Dorset.

The Cross stands thirty feet high and is believed to be of limestone from Marnhull or Todber.

The actual date of its building is unknown, but the following Legend of Galfridius de Mervin was reputedly written down in 1534, in a book entitled *Durotrigiana*, and reprinted in the *Salisbury and Winchester Journal* of 29th February 1768.

Galfridius de Mervin, Knight of Malta, was sorely rent and torn with dolorous wounds, in the victorious attack which this right valiant champion and likewise his brethen made upon the bloodie saracens in the year 1309.

Albeit when his friends had banished from their breasts all hope of recovery, Saint John, the tuterlarie saint of the order, appeared unto him at his bedside with a plugale of most miraculous unction, did forthwith anoynte and cure his blessures.

To make a meets return thereunto, he was ordered to erect a pillar, which was to be removed into the several countries where he might in future times set his mind to live and also to remain there during his stay. The saint likewise delivered a behest that an inscription be devised and graven on the said pillar.

He then prophecied that the knights of Malta should possess Rhodes without interruption untill the time should come when the said inscription should be suddenly obliterated. With these words the holy man vanished.

Galfridius de Mervin, succeeding to rich demesnes in England, passed over unto that kingdom and took the pillar with him. His sister, Elfrida, was there given in marriage to one of the right noble and ancient family of Audley, Lordes of the Manor of Stallebrigge. In this town Galfridius erected the said pillar.

It was the work of the famous artist Pietro di Colonna, the disciple of Pazzino. The emblems and rare devices portrayed upon the pillar are Saint John, a lyon treading upon a crescent, wrythes of laurell, a chevalieresse or female hospitaler and the armoryalle standard of Malta, to wit, a white cross in a field argent.

In the beginning of the year 1522, in the reign of Henry VIII the inscription became suddenly effaced, and incontinently, news was brought that through the treachery of the chancellor of the order, Rhodes was taken by Soloman the magnificent.

MCCCIX
GAL:D. MER: SAN:IOH:VUL:MED:
COL:RHOD:
PERIT: NUNQ: MAN:LITT:
P : L : M.

An interpretation of the figures would be as follows; the figure of St John appearing as Patron Saint of the Order. A lion treading on a crescent symbolized the Order crushing the Infidel; the banner would have been a white cross in a field Gules (red), the Arms of the Order, rather than a field argent.

The inscription may have been interpreted as:

Galfridius de Mervin of the Order of Saint John wishes that the Mediterranean Colony of Rhodes may never perish while the letters remain. PLM.

As is usual with Legends, credibility is gained when certain facts emerge as truth and this is the case here, but the weight of the inconsistencies unfortunately overshadows them.

1. Galfridius as a Knight of St John, may indeed have taken part in a battle of 1309. In 1308, the island of Rhodes was granted by the Emperor Emmanuel to the Order of the Knights of St John of Jerusalem. Not long after the settlement, Rhodes was besieged by the Sultan Othman.

2. The last desperate siege did take place in 1522 when the Knights left Rhodes for ever, finally defeated by the Turks.

3. In 1530, by special concession of the Pope and the Emperor, Charles V of Spain, the Island of Malta was ceded to the homeless Knights of St John and they became established there until 1798. The Knights of Malta were required to defend the island from frequent incursions of the Moors and the Turks, it becoming a bastion of defence for the Christians of Europe.)

4. Members of the Audley family were Lords of the Manor of Stalbridge, the last but one bearing the name of Mervyn.

5. Stalbridge is only four miles distant from Templecombe, once a training establishment of the Knights Templars, later taken over by the Knights of St John. This followed the enforced retreat from the Holy Land and the augmenting of revenues from the confiscated estates of the Knights Templars, their great rivals, suppressed 1305-1312.

The arguments against the legend are these:-

Galfridius could not have been named as a Knight of Malta until after 1530;

The armorial colours are somewhat confusing, the Knights of the Order of St John being forced to wear black capes with white crosses;

The Audleys were Lords of the Manor of Stalbridge from 1553 to 1636. They were descended from Adam de Aldithley or Audley, who lived in the time of Henry I (1100-1135), the first Baron, by writ being Nicholas Audley, who died in 1317.

The legend in *Durotrigiana* (1534) must have been written after 1530, to include the phrase (Knight of Malta), and it would appear to be too early for the Stalbridge connection with the Audley family unless there was a renting of the Stalbridge estate under the Abbots of Sherborne before the Dissolution in 1539.

In the opinion of the RCHM and of Pevsner, the Cross is from the latter part of the fifteenth century.

To accommodate the Legend, one can imagine that perhaps one part of the stone was brought back to England and incorporated in a smaller Cross that was replaced or extended in a later century.

To add further flame to the imaginative fire, there are records of an inn in Stalbridge, which was called The Sarazen's Head in 1619.

Galfridius was an alternative name for Geoffrey.

Christian Audley, daughter of George Touchet, Lord Audley, and brother of Mervyn, second Earl of Castlehaven, Lord of the Manor of Stalbridge until 1631, married . . . Mervyn, son of Admiral Mervyn of Hampshire.

Their son was called Audley Mervyn and died in 1675.

HUTCHINS

From the text it is obvious that Hutchins himself scrutinised the Cross for his first edition of the *History of Dorset*.

> 'It stands on a base of three octagonal steps, on top of which is a square block forming the base of the shaft, small semi-detached pillars on corners. On its panels are carved subjects with relief, very defaced.
>
> One would suggest the Lord's resurrection. On it rests the shaft, a solid block of Ham Hill stone. On one side of it the standing Saviour with a lamb? At his feet, supported on a square bracket by an angel's Head, and covered by a bold projecting ogg canopy.

The shaft is surmounted by an octagonal cap bearing four shields on one of which Hutchins thought he discerned a chevron or fess between three roses or escallops, the alternate faces being filled by angels.

On this cap is an open stone shrine of rich tabernacle work, on whose front is a rude carving of the Crucifixion, which may have been altered in modern times from a Coronation of the Virgin, the Crucifixion, with the usual figures of the

Virgin and St John on the opposite face.

The whole was crowned by a crocketed spire, and most likely a cross over all; but this last stage is now replaced by a modern restoration.

The engraving in Hutchins is by Basire, paid for by the master of the fellows of Corpus Christi College, Cambridge (see frontispiece illustration). Basire's engraving gives fine detailing, but if, as admitted, the carvings on the panels were then much defaced, we are still left with conjecture as to subject and symbolism intended by those early masons.

It is worth including the following paragraph, written by Rev. W.S. Swayne towards the end of the nineteenth century, recording the customs appertaining to the Cross which evidently went out of use just before his period of residence in Stalbridge.

Up to comparatively late years it was customary to illuminate the Cross with candles on the day of Shroton Fair. As lately as 1877 the Rev. C.H. Mayo of Long Burton remarked rivulets of candle grease still remaining on the upper portion of the Cross. It was generally supposed that the illumination was in honour of Shroton Fair. The true explanation, of course was that Shroton Fair was granted to be held on the Eve, Feast, and Morrow of the Exaltation of the Holy Cross, Sept 14th, and is still kept on the Sept 25th and 26th, i.e. the Festival and Morrow, old style.

Within the last ten years, the Cross has been reinforced at the base because of damage from vehicles and there has also been an attempt to have it moved in order to preserve it. Feelings have been mixed and the result is a very recent addition of a raised block approach to prevent further encroachment on the dignity of one of Stalbridge's oldest possessions.

NINE

Tudor Stalbridge

A very general picture of life in Stalbridge at the beginning of the sixteenth century can be gleaned from the Manor Court Roll of Abbot John Meere for 1515-1516. The area of land he controlled was a considerable part of north and west Dorset, and Stalbridge and Stalbridge Weston were mentioned as having a Hocktide Manor Court in May, 1515, but no Michaelmas Court that year, possibly through inaccessibility from Sherborne because of the weather.

At this Court, the Bailiff was ordered to distrain Thomas Thornhill of Thornhill to do feudal homage for lands etc. by military service of one quarter of a knight's fee. Tenants who owed suits (service to the Abbot) were also brought before the Court, the tithing-man making a notable presence there.

The Court dealt with leases and copyholds and listened to the grievances of tenants. At Weston, there was a hedge in dispute between Johanna Bragge and John Chamberlayne. Fines could be imposed by the Court for trespass, polluting of village streams by cottage privies, wandering pigs, overstocking of common pastures, and on tapsters for selling ales without licence, millers for taking more than their due share of flour for grinding villagers' corn, and bakers could be fined 3d for selling loaves under the standard weight.

From the Ordinances read before the end of every Court, we can learn of the Court laws which set out the customary rights within the manor. Owners could be fined for putting sheep to feed on the stubble before all the corn had been carried away; no tenant could throw stones gathered from his acre-strip on to the acre-strips of his neighbours; cattle were not allowed to graze on the herbage that grew between the acre-strips when land was under cultivation; thorns, briars and gorse were to be removed from the common of pasture.

Of particular interest to 'Staplebridge' is the record in 1516 of rotation of crops in the area revealed in the payment by John Poskyn, Rector of Stalbridge Church, and Hugh Chylles for a land holding in South Field of the manor. They paid a fine of 40s for the joint-entry of land and 6s 8d in advance for the year when South Field was sown under wheat, and the same when it was sown under oats and barley, they being allowed to cultivate their strips from the Feast of St. Luke the Evangelist (18th Oct) until the Feast of St. Peter's Chains (1st Aug); the third year when the South Field was lying fallow, there was nothing to pay.

From the general description, it would seem that most cottages in the Roll were timber-framed and thatched, stone tiling being mentioned only once.

TAX RETURNS 1525

The Tax Returns for 1525 show that a considerable number of households were being maintained in the Stalbridge Tithing; the number of those taxed in Stalbridge was 50, and for Weston 26, Gomersay and Thornhill holding relatively small numbers of dwellings.

STALBRYGE TITHING

John Jenes	John Drege	Richard Baker
William Duffett	William Lockett	Richard Cowdrey
Thomas Attewater	John Lockett	John Clement
John Lock	Thomas Gawler	Richard Lyne
John Rabbatt	Walter Maynard	Agnes Lyghtfote wid
Hugh Galpyn	William Rabbatt	. . . .
John Bastabyll	William Tylden	Thomas Bentt
Walter Combe	Thomas Hyckes	Richard Snoke
William Stacy	William Downe	. . . Geffrey
Edmund Hoper	John Derby	
Hugh Duffett	William Combe	John Corny (cke?)
Bartholomew Haykyns	Thomas . . . yckeson	John Sherd
Richard Hoper	Thomas . . . f	William Rabbatt
Hugh Chyldes	William Strang	John Bastabyll jun
Thomas Kyng	Margaret Dogpole	John Moleyns
Agnes Anturne	Thomasina Goslyng	John Troutell
Thomas Anturne	John Fugge	William Galpyn
John Davage	William Foster	John Galpyn
Henry Gauterell	William Chyles	Richard Hawkyns
Total £4 4s 1d		

WESTON TITHING 1525

Margaret Weston wid	Edith Hoper wid	Thomas Lock
William Weston	John Baylly	William Chamberlayne
William Chamberlayn	Alianora Lymyn wid	William Grove
William Locke	Humphry Milward	Richard Gauterell
William Chyldes	William Snoke	Robert Gauterell
Margaret Lymyn wid	Richard Snoke	Henry Brage
Richard Lymyn	William Lock jun	Henry Toocker
John Chyldes	Thomas Snoke	John Chyles jun
Margaret Snoke wid	William Peers	
Total £2 18s 6d		

GOMERSHEY TITHING

Richard Ryggeley	Thomas Wrigley	William Chyles
John Ryggeley	John Chyles	
Total £1 9s 10d		

THORNHULL TITHING

Thomas Thornhull	John Rownde	John Fry
William Sherley	Richard Creych	John Snoke
John Wheler	Richard Snoke	John Snoke
William Hyll	John Pavyett	John Galpyn
Total £4 6s 2d		

LELAND'S DESCRIPTION OF STALBRIDGE

The first description of Stalbridge's linear development is from Leland's visit in the 1530s.

He came upon the town from the direction of Master Carent's house at Toomer;

'From Stourton on to . . . (probably Kington Magna) four miles much by woddy ground. Here I passed over Cale Water at a greate ford, and so ryde scant a mile over moreland, and a myle beyond I left . . . Master Corfent's (Carent's) howse and parke on the lefte hande; and thens a mile farther, I came on to Stapleford, a praty uplandisch toune of one streate, meately well buildyd, where at the northe end of the town is a churche;

The lordship and townelet of Stapleford in Blakemore hath longgid of auncient tyme unto the abbay of Shirburne. Cale ryver cummith downe from Moreland unto Stapleford, leaving it on the righte rype (bank).

Stapleforde is by estimation 7 miles N. of Wikehampton and Wincaunton, from whens Cale brooke cummeth. From Tonmer (Toomer) to Stalbridge a myle.

This towne was privilegyd with a market and faire, by the procurement of an abbat of Sherburne. The market is decayed. The fair remaynithe. The Abbot of Shireburne, lorde of the towne, had there a maner place on the southe side of the church. There is a right goodly spring on the south side of the church, waullyd about. Stour is the next water on it, and that levith Stalbridge about a mile on the right ripe. Cale Bridge on Cale Ryver is a mile and halfe off.'

From this description, one can determine the pattern of Stalbridge's one street, well defined and 'meately well buildyd.' The base foundations of many dwellings down Church Hill and along the High Street must have first been laid during the medieval period.

It is noted that the Abbot of Sherborne also had a manor place, 'on the south side of the church.' Was this the 'capital messuage' of 1350, and was it close to the church or on church land around the Cross, on which the new rectory was built in 1699?

Leland does not mention the Stalbridge Cross, which, if correctly dated belongs to the late fifteenth century, should have been extraordinarily beautiful with its remarkable carvings not more than fifty years old when he visited the town.

TUDOR MUSTER ROLLS

Defending one's country in peacetime nowadays is a voluntary career; compulsory National Service, except in an emergency, would be considered an imposition. Yet until Waterloo, men had been trained for the defence of their country and were enrolled for the Militia, from amongst able-bodied men in the town and village.

From 1446, when an Act of Parliament declared that longbows matching the height of every able-bodied Englishman should be held in readiness for emergencies, parishes had their clusters of men who no doubt practised at the Butts, Stalbridge being no exception. It is from the Tudor Muster Rolls that we find an impressive list of Stalbridge men ready to use the weapons of war, namely the pike, the bow and the billaxe.

According to some writers, skill in archery and the obligation to serve in the militia had fostered a spirit of independence, regarded as 'peculiarly English.' In the later Middle Ages, there was

'. . . almost no village so poor in England . . . that it hath not sufficient furniture in a readiness to set forth three or four soldiers, as one archer, one gunner, one pike and a billman, at the least. The said armour and munition is kept in one several place appointed by the consent of the whole parish, where it is always ready to be had and worn within an hour's warning.'

Stalbridge had a considerable corps of 58 men enrolled in 1539, the same number as in 1569; the same three men in each Roll, although 30 years apart, remained entitled to handle one of the more advanced weapons, the harquebus, an awkward type of shot, standing on a tripod.

From the Rolls, one can note the blossoming of surnames that show the differences between the Lay Subsidy Rolls of two hundred years previously and the sixteenth century. They are more familiar to our modern ears and include some names which have come down to present generations.

As well as harquebuzers, there were in readiness in Stalbridge, pikemen, billmen, and archers.

STAWBRIDGE TITHING 1539

HARQUEBUZERS
John Galley gent   Mich Huchins.

PIKEMEN

Tho Snowke	Jn Turner	Wm Duffet	Wm Hickes	Jn Townesende
Adrian Peter	Hen Bushe	Phil Parsons	Jn Michell	Wm Townesende
Wm Flower	Geo Frye	Jn Snowk jun	Jn Barstable	

BILLMEN

Wm Jeanes	Hen Snowke	Nic Ordre	Ambrose Bestly	Jn Courtney
Rob Balston	Jn Carter	Jn Cryer	Jn Kelwaye	Jn Snowke sen
Jn Osmonde	Jn Lock jun	Jn Wattes	Jn Paradyze	Jn Roberts jun
Huch Huchins	Bob Bushe	Simon Abbott		

ARCHERS

Wm Browne	Jn Lucke	Bart Duffet	Geo Geanes	Reyn Bernard
Edm Golde	Jn Kinge	Rob Derbye	Wm Haskel	Ric Glover
Bart Myles				

STAWBRIDGE WESTON

PIKEMAN	Wm Gawtrell	
BILLMAN	Rob Kember	
ARCHERS	Ric Gaunt	Jn Turner

THORNHEHYLL AND GOMERSEY

HORSEMAN	Rob Thornehyll Esq		
HARQUEBUZER	Tho Kelwaye		
PIKEMEN	Wm Hyll	Jn Sage	
BILLMEN	Jn Chalcott	Wm Genge	Ric Whytehed
ARCHERS	Jn Chyles	Geo Russell	

Comparing the 1539 Muster Roll with the 1543 tax lists, the names are the same, except for six names omitted from the list of taxpayers.

Looking at the 1543 tax lists (82 names) with the 1569 Muster Roll, at a distance in time which precluded the men on the former Muster Roll of 1539 because of age and possible decease, one finds several new surnames in the lists. This could of course mean the growing up to the age of military service of new families, but it could also mean an injection of new blood and shifting population, either an increase in the number of able-bodied servants from elsewhere, or an increase in the livelihoods that supported new families moving into Stalbridge, and therefore new growth in the town itself.

1569 MUSTER ROLL

STAWBRIDGE TITHING

H Jn Galley gent	A Geo Geanes	B Jn Osmonde	B Nic Ordre
P Tho Snowke	H Mich Huchins	B Jn Snowke sen	A Rob Derbye
B Wm Jeanes	B Jn Keylwaye	P Jn Barstable	B Jn Wattes
B Hen Snowke	B Rob Balston	P Wm Flower	B Ambrose Bestly
P Jn Turner	A Edm Golde	P Geo Frye	A Wm Haskel
P Wm Duffett	P Adrian Peter	B Jn Locke jun	B Rob Bushe
B Jn Courteney	P Hen Bushe	A Ric Glover	A Bart Duffett
A Wm Browne	P Phil Parsons	B Jn Roberts jun	P Jn Michell
A Jn lucke	P Jn Townsende	B Jn Paradyze	A Bart Myles
A Reyn Bernard	A Jn Kinge	B Hugh Huchins	B Jn Cryer

48

P Wm Hickes   B Jn Carter   B Simon Abbott
P Jn Snowk jun   P Wm Townsende

STAWBRIDGE WESTON
P Wm Gawtrell   A Jn Turner   B Rob Kember   A Ric Gaunt

THORNEHYLL AND GOMERSEY
Ho Rob Thornehyll Esg   P Jn Sage   B Wm Genge
H Tho Keylwaye   A Jn Chyles B Ric Whytehed   P Wm Hyll
B Jn Chalcot   A Geo Russell

DISSOLUTION OF THE MONASTERIES

One of the consequences for Stalbridge of the Dissolution of the Monasteries was a change of rector. John Barnstable, last Abbot of Sherborne Abbey, became rector and stayed for twenty years, and on his death was buried in the chancel of Stalbridge Church.

Stalbridge also had a new owner to whom they paid their rents, the King's uncle, the Duke of Somerset. He did not remain long; attainted in 1553, he was followed by members of the Touchet family.

The coming of the Touchets must point speculative fingers at the coincidence of the names, e.g. Mervyn and Audley, which arose in connection with the legends of the Cross. Whether the Touchets continued to live in the manor house on the south side of the church, as described by Leland, can only be conjecture. Unfortunately, little remains of the architecture of this period to look for possible sites.

TEN

The Manor of Stalbridge

After the Dissolution of the Monasteries, the Sherborne Abbey Estates were dispersed, and the manor, advowson and lands of Stalbridge were granted by Edward VI in 1547 to the Duke of Somerset, the King's uncle and Lord Protector of England. Amidst great rivalry from Warwick and opposing factions, Somerset allowed the execution of his own brother, Thomas Seymour, once married to Catherine Parr, Henry VIII's widow, and not entirely innocent of depriving the Crown of revenues, to proceed without trial. He was in turn deposed as Lord Protector and executed in 1552.

On his attainder, the Stalbridge estate passed to John Touchet. Lord Audley, and heirs male, 'to be held of the King in chief by Knight's service, paying yearly £28.1s.3d.' His ancestor, James, seventh Lord Audley, disaffected after giving support to the Lancastrians in the Civil War, and support, without recognition, to Henry VII's cause at Boulogne, joined the Cornishmen's Rising in 1497, was caught, and executed.

In 1562, it was Henry, son and heir of George Touchet, who held the manor of Stalbridge, valued at £70. Twelve years later in 1574, George, Henry's son, inherited the estate in whose hands it remained until 1618.

At the Visitation of Dorsetshire in 1565, two families were noted, the Galle family, who were lessees of the Audleys, leasing land and possibly a house, and the Keilweys. John Galle was from Stalbridge but his father and grandfather came from Whitnell, Somerset.

William Keilwey, (son of Thomas Keilwey of Sherborne), married as his first wife, Elizabeth Whiffen of 'Stawbridge'; his son, Thomas of Stawbridge, married Margarett Martin of Athelhampton.

Because of the intense political involvements of the Lord Protector, it is not likely that he gave more than a passing thought to his minor estate in Dorset; nor could the first Audleys, owners of large estates elsewhere, have given much attention to Stalbridge if they let it to the Gales.

Stalbridge was granted to Mervyn, Lord Audley in 1618, on the death of his father, George, Lord Audley, who had been created first Earl of Castlehaven.

According to Coker, it was Mervyn, Lord Audley, second Earl of Castlehaven, who built a 'goodlie faire house' in Stalbridge, but only after a legal battle.

When Mervyn, Lord Audley, son of George Touchet, inherited the estate and wished to build his house on land near the Church, the voice of the inhabitants was heard claiming rights they deemed theirs in a legal suit they endeavoured to bring against their Lord of the Manor.

The building of the house could only take place after the conclusion of the Chancery suit in 1618, brought by the inhabitants protesting against the loss of common rights on 'a great pasture and waste and wooddy ground'. The attempt by Mervyn at enclosure of 'common' land and the strength of the protest showed the dependence on the higher land around the church above the marshy levels liable to flooding to the east and south of Stalbridge.

The Earl of Castlehaven had approached the 42 copyholders of Stalbridge, 29 of whom decided to take rights of common elsewhere and 13 to take a money payment, but had not sought agreement with the 18 copyholders of Sir George Thornhill's manor of Stalbridge Weston and the farmer of Antioch, who stirred the other tenants to dispute the enclosure.

The case was a lengthy one in which the tenants claimed that the common provided fern for their tenements, furze for baking and brewing, and pasturage for their cattle and sheep, and that without it they could not 'soyle and manure their areable lands and paie their rents'.

The tenants eventually lost their claim and the Earl built his manor house to the north-west of St. Mary's Church and enclosed several acres of land immediately surrounding it. This large house, built imposingly slightly north-west of St. Mary's Church, ranked as the fifth largest house in Dorset. The size of the impressive mansion, with its huge mullioned windows, stepped gables and tall, ornate chimneys, can be seen in the engraving entitled 'Stalbridge House' in Hutchins' *History of Dorset* (see plate section in this book).

From details shown in a later map, the old Stalbridge Park, enclosed by Mervyn, contained only about fifty acres, not the 500 acres that were enclosed within the five mile wall built by another Lord of the Manor, Edward Walter, during the eighteenth century.

Evidence that Mervyn, Lord Audley, lived in his 'goodlie faire house' is given in a suit in 1639 concerning a bequest of £100 to the poor of Stalbridge in the Will of his brother, Sir Ferdinando Tutchett, (sic), Knt. deceased, second son of George, first Earl of Castlehaven, co. Cork. It states that

'Sir Ferdinando had lived with his brother, the (second) Earl of Castlehaven at Stalbridge who was lord of the town and manor of Stalbridge and had received part of his education in the town.'

John Jeanes 'Tayler', of Stalbridge, aged 46 in 1639, had been a 'scholler' with Tutchett in the town of Stalbridge.

Mervyn's eldest son was James, who succeeded him; his second son, George, born at Stalbridge, became a monk, making his solemn profession in the English Benedictine Monastery of St. Gregory at Douay in 1643. By Act of Parliament in 1678, George was excluded from the succession to the earldom of Castlehaven.

It is not possible to confirm whether James, like his younger brother,

George, was also born in Stalbridge; the oldest Stalbridge Parish Register was quoted by Hutchins, but in 1869 it was deemed to be lost. James's education had been utterly neglected and from subsequent events, it would seem that the circumstances of his family life, made him very unhappy. He was married when he was a boy of thirteen or fourteen to Elizabeth Brydges, daughter of his father's second wife, Anne, by her first husband, Grey Brydges. The girl herself had been forced into criminal intercourse by her stepfather, when only twelve, with her mother's paramour, Skipwith.

James became so disgusted at the 'scenes of bestiality he was compelled to witness', that he appealed to the King for protection from Mervyn, his own father. The consequence for Mervyn was a state trial at Westminster on 5th April 1631

'for abetting Rape upon his Countess Committing Sodomy with his servants and Commanding and Countenancing the Debauching of his Daughter.'

He was found guilty, consigned to the gallows and beheaded on Tower Hill.

After the attainder of his father, James was able to recover the English title in 1633, the Irish peerage being preserved against forfeiture, but most of his father's estates in England passed into other hands.

ELEVEN

A Goodlie Faire House, 1636-1699

The Earl of Cork, who bought the Stalbridge estate from James, Earl of Castlehaven, in 1636, was already acquainted in Ireland with the Touchet family. The Countess of Castlehaven, wife of Mervyn, second Earl of Castlehaven, had been godmother to the Earl's fourteenth child, Robert Boyle, who was born in 1627 at Lismore Castle, rebuilt by Sir Walter Ralegh in the sixteenth century before it came later into the possession of the Earl of Cork.

Appointed Lord Treasurer of Ireland in 1631 and much occupied in the 1630's in building and fortifying houses in Ireland for his older sons and two daughters, the Earl of Cork paid £5,000 for the Dorset manor, advowson and lands, later acquiring other properties around Stalbridge for a further £2,085.

Unable to come to Dorset for two years after buying his English estate, the Earl was kept informed by his Stalbridge steward, Thomas Crosse, and details from the Earl of Cork's Letter Book, 1634-1641, and the Lismore MSS, reveal not only the masons' asking prices but also the Earl's final, and often lower, offer, suggesting his shrewd business acumen and interest.

The Earl's architect for the alterations to the Manor House, said to have been in great decay when the Earl became the owner, is believed to have been Isaac de Caux, but from the precise descriptions given below, the monumental scale of the additions suggest the hand of the Earl himself.

For his new 'intended bwylding' over the great cellar in Stalbridge, the Earl made an agreement with Walter Hyde, a Sherborne mason

'to make and sett up . . . 4 wrought chymneis, with Figures answerable or better than the chymney in my own bed-chamber, of stoan of Marnell quarrey'.

He was insistent that Walter Hyde should obtain 'hambdon' stone for 'eight Rownd Pillars with capitalls and Bases a foot long set up in the cellar' to 'lay beames' of his 'firste Flowers vppon', and to dig out of Hambden quarry 'soe much good stone' for the 'Rayles, bases, Balasters and peddistalls' between his 'owtwarde' gate and the hall door, and the 'Tarras' before his hall door, from wall to wall, 'being in all that is soe to be rayled in about 300 foot'; the 'balasters' to be set

'soe neer and close together, that a dog cannot not creep between.'

The great beam 24 feet long 'to lay in the Flowr vnder the great chamber at Stalbridge', cost the Earl forty shillings.

He had obviously been to the Earl of Bristol's house in Sherborne, because he wished to have the paving between his 'owt-moste gate' to his hall door and the Terrace, of 'Rangerpavies' of Freestone, from the same vein of hard Freestone as that paving the Earl's Courtyard.

The cost of carriage was to be paid by the Earl of Cork, who was to pay Gregory Brimsmead, the Earl of Bristol's free mason, at a rate of 'three pence halfe penney the foot.'

The same mason was also paid 'for making the staire case owt of my little court in Stalbridge.'

The Earl's descriptions of the work he required show much concern not only for the cost of the individual pieces of work but also reflect his very definite ideas for the appearance, quality and effect of the differing types of stone.

Christopher Watts of Bristol, mason and carver, was to make 'a very fair chymney' for the parlour to reach up 'close to the seeling', as the Earl carefully outlined, with

'Coat of Armes compleate, with crest, Helmett, Coronett, Supporters and mantling, and foot pace . . . and also 12 Fygures, each 3 foot highe, to sett upon . . . the staircase, for which he demaunds 20s a peece, & I offer him 13s.4d. and he is presently to cutt one of them with the figure of pallace with a sheeld; one with my coat with a corronet is to be cutt for a tryall.'

This must be the staircase described by Hutchins in his *History of Dorset* as having figures of the twelve apostles about a yard high placed at intervals between the balusters.

The House in Stalbridge Park contained startling modern innovations, as it was complete with plumbing arrangements three hundred years ahead of most of the dwellings in Stalbridge. There were 'boylers, gwtters, pipes', and a 'plump cestern' included in the payment of £40 which the Earl made 'in full satisfaction' to John Dean, plumber of Sherborne, for the lead, 'sawder and worckmanship, daie labours and all other demaunds for the plomer worcks' done at the Stalbridge house. The work included leaden pipes to carry water to 'Severall vnder Roomes' in the house.

The Earl added a bowling green, a popular meeting place for gentlemen of the period, which was made 'by a noseles man, named Thomas Ford,' and he wrote approvingly of a Stalbridge mason, John Hopkins, who

'added one Round Staier more at the lower part of my stone staires ascending to my outward gate there; and . . . a dry stone wall of 2 foot thick and 9 foot highe, from my brew howse to the gate of the lane going to sherborn; . . . he making the stone-wall neatly, strong, and worckmanleyke.'

The Earl of Cork further improved the park around the Manor House by acquiring from Sara Eyres for £5, the 'sope boyler's' cottage and garden, adjoining the orchard wall, so that he could lengthen the walk, or 'carreer by me, newly made and sett with yonge elmes, called Wm Sidnam's walck.'

It is likely that the Earl's taste for grandeur led him to finish off his new 'carreer' with the imposing lion figureheads set on massive gate piers, which still adorn the entrance to Stalbridge Park.

The lions, which according to local tradition occasionally come off their pedestals at night to prowl, still survive as seventeenth century sentinels to the Park, and echo the lions in the Boyle crest adorning the family monument, erected by the Earl of Cork, at Youghal.

The Earl of Cork did not neglect the domestic arrangements, for the garden was stocked with new fruit trees and the Earl of Bristol's son-in-law, Mr Freke, sent forty young apple trees and twelve grafted pear trees, 'Bonchrittens and Burgoyncs'. William Cutler was the Earl of Cork's gardener, beginning his apprenticeship for five years with a 'suit of apparel and three pounds wages'.

In 1640, the Earl was having a wall built in his garden and fruit trees were being offered by Goodman Higgins of Westbury. A bill for seeds included Hotspur Peas, Dutch Beans and Sandwich Peas.

The next year saw works still going on at Stalbridge, but a new property was added to the Earl's estate, being that at Annecy, Devon, 'one of the goodliest homes in the western parts of England'. It was said that the Earl could put his foot into a boat at Youghal and land at his own door. A letter from Thomas Murray one month later gives an account of a visit to Marston Bigot, which the Earl had previously bought for his son, Roger.

When the Countess of Warwick came to stay in Stalbridge House with her father, she made timely notes in her diary which gives us some indication of the style of living in the Cork household.

The Earl left his housekeeping to his married daughter, Alice Barrymore, and his daughter-in-law, Lady Dungarvan, but did not fail to notice when their thrift was not as keen as his own, he finding that they were in debt to bakers, brewers, vintners and graziers to the sum of £700, repaying the sums with ready money 'for the preservation of their credits and mine in this country'.

On another occasion, anxious to keep his reputation, he was required to pay a Southampton merchant eighteen pounds for a ton of claret wine, which should have been paid out of his daughters' housekeeping allowance of £50 a week.

This magnificent Stalbridge House must have been an awesome sight for the traveller approaching Stalbridge from Somerset. Yet twice within five years it was to house the forces fighting for the King and it must be presumed that some of them encamped in Stalbridge Park around the Earl's mansion.

It is hardly likely that in the presence of the Earl, who had spent so much time and thought on his masterpiece, and even kept his gardens locked, that they would be allowed to misuse his great house, when in May 1639, men and horses were quartered in Stalbridge.

On 4th May 1639, Lord Dungarvon's waggon and carriages began their journey from Stalbridge to the north. Late that night, Dick Power, Cornet of the Horse Troop, reached Stalbridge ahead of the horsemen and horses newly arrived at Minehead from Ireland. The Troop took another three days before it entered Stalbridge on 7th May.

For two days, men and horses were quartered in Stalbridge. The presence of so many strangers, the hustle and activity of feeding alone, as well as the excitement of the anticipated departure and long march north must have left a long impression on the inhabitants as much as on the sensitive, youngest son of the Manor.

The Earl of Cork wrote in his diary:

'9 May 1639. This daie . . . my three sons, the Lord Dongarvan, Kynalmeakie and Broghill, with the troop of one hundredth horse that I supplied my son dongarvan with moneis to raise, buy, and arme, to serve his Maty withall against his rebillows Scottish Subjects, departed from me at Stalbridge.'

Not many weeks afterwards, Broghill returned on Midsummer Day, 1639, arriving in Stalbridge at 2 o'clock in the morning, with the glad news that peace was restored with the Scots.

The finances which supported the Earl's expenses of the Stalbridge Manor House, indentured for his youngest son, Robert, in 1640, came mainly from his Irish estates. The Earl and several members of his family, however, were unable to enjoy the modern improvements to the large mansion for more than a short period. Financial problems seemed to beset him from all quarters.

Lettice, one of the Earl's daughters, had become a sufferer of 'Grief and Melancholy', having a rake of a husband, George Goring, who had already borrowed £8,000 from his father-in-law (a tremendous sum by modern standards) and required another £500 to set them straight.

The Earl had generously given his oldest son, Lord Dungarvan, the means to fit out a company of Irish soldiers in 1639, some setting out from Stalbridge, to take up positions behind King Charles I in the North against the Scots.

The Earl had also given the King a loan of £15,000 but had unfortunately pressed for its return. Now, possibly due to personal grievance, Lord Deputy Wentworth was determined to get it back. Through a case based on the doubtful rights of the Earl to take rents and money dues from the College of Youghal in Ireland, the Lord Deputy was threatening to take the Earl of Cork to the Star Chamber unless he paid the fine of £15,000.

As if that wasn't enough to upset his equilibrium, the Great Rebellion was breaking out in Ireland in the middle months of the year 1641, and the Earl's estates were being plundered.

His two youngest sons, Francis and Robert Boyle had left for the Grand Tour in 1639, and could not return to England because a 'deceitful' friend had failed to send on their allowance, soon to be cut off altogether by the Earl's diminishing fortunes.

The Earl prepared to set out for Ireland but had to wait for a boat with a willing captain and also permission to sail.

There was one consolation before he had to leave his English possessions for the last time. His adversary, Wentworth, had found the tables turned against him in Parliament and had been beheaded in May 1641.

The Earl arrived to find the rents on his Irish estates no longer being paid, and in January, 1642, he wrote a letter declaring that when he arrived in Ireland, he had a rental of £20,000 but now could not get in his last year's rent as no man would 'part with a penny'.

His Protestant tenants rallied round the Earl and after many bloody skirmishes, a kind of restless peace was restored. With his oldest sons and sons-in-law engaged in the defence of the Irish properties in the Great Rebellion of 1641, the loss of financial resources due to the expenses of fitting out an army of Protestant tenants, put great strain on the Earl and his family. He wrote that before the Rebellion his rents provided £50 a day, but that afterwards he was taking not more than pence per day.

The Earl's son, Kinalmeaky, was shot in battle and had to be buried at Lismore, the Earl's Irish home in September 1642.

Nor was there any comfort in news from England. In 1642, the Civil War had broken out, families were divided in loyalties, even his own daughter, Katherine, had marriage ties with the Parliamentary side, although this may have saved the sequestration later of the Stalbridge estate.

By Christmas, 1642, the great Earl of Cork, had lost one son, found several of his sons and daughters with shattered Irish homes, was owed much money by his son-in-law, George Goring, and that which must have upset him most of all, had little contact with his favourite son, Robert Boyle, unable to leave Europe.

Yet his letters show a remarkable attention to estate business written until just two months before he died in September 1643. The Stalbridge House and lands had been indentured to his youngest son, Robert, now Lord of the Manor of Stalbridge but still stranded in Geneva with M. Marcombes.

TWELVE

The 'Father of Chemistry'

A fter spending part of the formative years of his youth in this North Dorset village, Robert Boyle inherited the Stalbridge Estate when his father died, and it is not generally realised that he was Lord of the Manor of Stalbridge for nearly fifty years until his death in 1691.

Born in Lismore, Ireland, on 27th January 1627, into the wealthy family of the 'Great' Earl of Cork, Robert, the fourteenth child of the Earl's second wife, was not allowed to indulge himself in the luxuries of a home in the fortified castle of Lismore. His father, Richard Boyle, once a solicitor's clerk in London, although acquiring wealth through two successive marriages in Ireland, believed that Robert should become acclimatised "to a coarse but cleanly diet and the usual passions of the air," by living out with an Irish nurse. Robert returned home when he was five, by which time his mother had died, and he was given tuition in reading, writing, Latin and French before being sent to Eton with his older brother, Francis.

Crossing the Irish Sea at that time presented a hazard for the young travellers, equally as dangerous as the storm which forced their boat to return to harbour at Youghal and caused another eight days' delay. During the seventeenth century, when Dutch fishing vessels encroached in British waters to the annoyance of the local fishermen and Dunkirk pirates were proving a hazard to ships leaving southern ports, Turkish galleys also roamed the seas in search of captives taken from ships along the English and Irish coasts to be sold as slaves in the Mediterranean.

Briefs in several Dorset Parish Registers reflect a concern and reveal the misery of fear in coastal villages from the marauders from the sea. In the small mid-Dorset village of Winterborne Houghton, five pence was given for 'ye ransoming ye captives in Algiers and Sally . . . ' and later, '. . . for ye ransoming ye captives out of Turkey 5 shillings six pence coll(ected) Nov 4. 1670.'

Robert and his brother were fortunate, for, he wrote later, '. . . the Irish Coasts were then sufficiently infested with Turkish Gallyes . . .', but the boys' ship touched unharmed at Ilfracombe and Minehead, before landing at Bristol.

Robert and his brother spent four years at Eton, during which time they had sufficient alarms to make them thankful for miraculous escapes.

When the wall of their bedchamber fell down, and that of the room above them, Francis, sitting by the fireside, was snatched away from the scene by a 'lusty Youth', and Robert in bed, was saved by the thick bed curtains and the sheet, which 'strained' the purer air from all the dust of the 'Crumbled rubbish', which otherwise would have stifled him.

On one occasion when Robert fell from his horse, the beast ran over him and trod so close to his throat to make a hole in his neck 'band'. Robert's presence of mind in throwing himself to the ground when his horse took fright and reared, avoided him being crushed against a wall. He escaped with only a slight bruise.

The retirement of their tutor, Mr Harrison, who had been a great inspiration for Robert, particularly, and the unreliability of their trusted servant, Carew, may have been reasons for the Earl withdrawing his sons from Eton in 1638.

The Earl left Stalbridge with the boys on 9th October 1638, and dropped them at Eton on 11th October, on his way to London. Returning to Stalbridge from London on Friday, 23rd November, the Earl had finally decided to discontinue their education at this prestigious establishment, and called at Eton and removed his sons from the college and brought them back to Stalbridge.

Stalbridge House, which had been greatly refurbished by the Earl, was visited by various members of the large family, but in order to avoid the 'temptations to idlenesse' in the Stalbridge household, Robert was sent to live with the Parson, Rev. William Douch, 'tho it were not distant . . . above twice musket-shot,' where he learnt to speak Latin with reasonable fluency and to write verses in French, Latin and English. Most of his early poems, Robert later burnt on his 21st birthday.

When two of Robert's older brothers arrived in Stalbridge, having completed the Grand Tour of Europe, Robert was taken back into the family home and placed under the care of their tutor, M. Marcombes.

Robert was also taught some skill in music, 'both of the Voyce/song/ & hand;' but found some discouragement in having a 'Bad Voyce'.

In 1639, the Earl decided to send Robert, accompanied by Francis, to join the three older brothers on a Scottish Expedition with King Charles. Robert saw the preparations for dispatching forces which took place in Stalbridge, and eagerly looked forward to accompanying them, his eldest brother, Lord Dungarvon, readily supporting King Charles I by

'hauing at his owne Charges rais'd a Gallant Troope of Horse for the King's seruice in the Scotch Expedition.'

It had been the Earl's intention to send Robert with his older brother, Francis, who, being ill, was unable to travel, thus denying Robert an experience of the field of battle, although presumably not one of participation.

This adventure had come to nought for Robert and he wrote that his 'greedy hopes' were thus 'defeated'. Instead, he was given the key of all his father's garden and orchards at Stalbridge.

Robert believed that his father was obliging him to be temperate by 'freely giving him the Opportunity to be otherwise'. But the boy had evidently no fancy for sweetmeats and 'in Fruite' he was 'very moderate'.

When resting from his studies, he liked to steal away from company and

'spend 4 or 5 howres alone in the fields, to (walk) about, & thinke at Random; making his delighted Imagination the busy Scene, where some Romance or other was dayly acted . . .'

This idyll, however, was soon to be cut short, for the family travelled to London for the marriage arranged between fifteen-year old Francis and Elizabeth, step-daughter of Sir Thomas Stafford, a gentleman usher to the Queen, with King Charles I giving away the bride.

Only four days after the wedding, the Earl of Cork ordered the bridegroom, Francis, and the younger Robert, with a licence giving the King's permission to travel abroad for three years, to set out on a European tour with M. Marcombes as tutor. Travelling through France, Switzerland and Italy, they were in Florence when Galileo died, but the brothers had to cut short their tour when grave misfortunes at home affected their financial status.

The three oldest sons of the Earl were engaged with their father in helping to quell the Great Rebellion in Ireland in 1641, which required the Earl to use his wealth in providing a Protestant army to defend his family's estates in Munster. The subsequent loss of income meant the loss of the generous allowance for the younger boys' travel.

Because of this misfortune and the lamentable fact that Mr Perkins, entrusted by the Earl of Cork to send on the last allowance of £250 for Robert and his brother, had failed to do so, the future of Robert Boyle may have been very different.

Unable to return with Francis to the fighting in Ireland, in which their older brother, Lewis (Kinalmeaky), was killed, Robert stayed with M. Marcombes in Geneva. The untimely death of the Earl followed on 15th September, 1643, which lengthened Robert's stay in Geneva until funds were available for his return to England in 1644 as Lord of the Manor of Stalbridge, inheriting from his father the estate which had been conveyed to him by indenture on 30th November, 1640, two months before his fourteenth birthday.

RETURN TO STALBRIDGE

Robert Boyle arrived at his 'ruined cottage in the country', in 1644, a well-seasoned traveller, using the French tongue as a native. Whilst abroad, he had spent some months fencing and was also used to travelling with a 'kaise of pistoles' at his side because it was 'so much the mode for every gentleman of fashion', and a sword.

Yet in spite of all the inconveniences and greater hazards of travel, much heightened by the Civil War, during the next eleven years when he used Stalbridge as his main home, he was frequently absent.

By the time of his arrival around the end of 1644, the northern part of the county of Dorset had already experienced some of the turmoil and strife of the War, and King Charles and his army had encamped in Stalbridge on the night of Tuesday, 8th October 1644.

It is not certain whether Robert Boyle had left London by this time to be able to act as host to the King, whom he had already met in London at the wedding of his brother, Francis.

The fact that Symonds wrote in his diary that the King 'lay that night at Stawbridge, the faire house of the Earl of Corke' suggests that the ownership of the house by Robert Boyle was not fully realised.

There was a further family connection with the army because the Royalist Commander of the forces in the South West was Robert's brother-in-law, George Goring, a rakish character, who had borrowed large sums of money from his father-in-law, the Earl of Cork.

Robert Boyle arrived in London from Geneva 'towards the middle of the year 1644.' He stayed there 'four months and a half', which places a doubt on the possibility of his being in Stalbridge before the middle of October to receive the King, and a letter, undated, written to Robert's steward of the manor of Stalbridge during the last quarter of 1644, would also seem to deny this.

In London, Robert found his sister, Lady Katherine Jones, who had fled from Ireland, and was living with a sister-in-law, whose husband was one of the leading members of the Presbyterian Party in the House of Commons.

Robert himself wrote of the advantages of living in a religious household. He argued that if a 'gracious Providence' had not detained him there, he would have been exposed to 'manifold and great temptations of a Court and an Army', notwithstanding the excellent King and eminent divines and many worthy Persons,

'. . . yet the generality of those he would have been oblig'd to converse wth were very debaucht & apt, as well as inclinable to make others so.'

Robert freely admitted the standing of those persons he met through his sister, for

'. . . by this means he grew acquainted wth several Persons of power & interest in ye Parliam^t and their party, wch being then very great, & afterwards the prevailing one, prov'd of good use, & advantage to him, in reference to his estate and concerns both in England and Ireland.'

It is clear from this statement that the connections through Katherine, Lady Ranelagh, whose sister-in-law's husband represented the Presbyterian Party in Parliament, probably saved the Stalbridge Estate, and consequently Stalbridge's Manor House from the despoilations of the Parliamentarians.

The Earl of Cork had clearly identified with the Royalist cause in 1639 and in Ireland in 1641, and King Charles had stayed in Stalbridge House in 1644.

The dilemma of the Boyle family must have increased when, later in the decade, Robert's brother, Broghill, was detained on a Royalist mission and taken to Cromwell, who drafted him under threat into the Parliamentary cause against the Irish.

There is no evidence of Robert's political activity nor indication of bias or sympathy, not even with the rising of the Clubmen in August 1645, although it is likely that Robert was in France during August of that year.

The same dilemma affected John Evelyn, later to become a friend of Robert and Trustee of the Boyle Lectures. He was another young man straining to be loyal to the King, yet uncertain of his own future in those doubtful days, which can be seen from a few extracts in his diary –

'1642 . . . joined the army for a few days'.

He left, he reasoned, because the ruin of him and his brother would not save the King.

In July 1643, he could not sign the Covenant, and being pressed he 'absented' himself. After obtaining a licence, he travelled abroad for several years, an equally hazardous project because of the Thirty Years' War on the Continent, finally returning home during the stabilised period of the Commonwealth.

During 1645, many Dorset estates close to Stalbridge were sequestered, but Robert continued to occupy his Manor House, not perhaps without some difficulty, occasionally expressed in his letters.

Writing from Stalbridge in March 1646, Robert Boyle, obviously aware of happenings in the countryside around him, wrote complainingly,

'My stay here, God willing, shall not be long, this country being generally infected with three epidemical diseases (besides that old leiger sickness, the troop-flux) namely the plague which now begins to revive again at Bristol and Yoevil (sic) six miles off, fits of the committee and consumption of the purse.'

Circumstances such as the taxes of the Standing Committee of 1646, and 'consumption of the purse', must have been much on his mind that year. His brother, Richard, Earl of Cork, had to compound for his estate, the fine fixed at £1,631.

In reply later to a request for employment from M. Marcombes, Robert, writing from London, could offer nothing, except advice to stay away from the miseries here,

'where every day presents us with much more unusual dispensations of providence, where I myself have been fain to borrow money of servants, to lend it to men of above £10,000 a year.'

The difficulty of his situation, which may explain his silence on the political questions, is revealed to M. Marcombes;

'I was once a prisoner here upon some groundless suspicions, but quickly got off with advantage . . . I have been forced to observe a very great caution, and exact evenness in my carriage, since I saw you last, it being absolutely necessary for the preservation of a person, whom the unfortunate situation of his fortune made obnoxious to the injuries of both parties, and the protection of neither.'

Robert was giving only a veiled glimpse of a vexing problem, about which, he had obviously been driven to take the measures he thought necessary to preserve his equilibrium. It was as much as he could reveal to anyone, M. Marcombes having been his tutor and known him under the most difficult circumstances in his developing youth.

THE STALBRIDGE SCIENTIST

It may be that the circumstances described somewhat guardedly to M. Marcombes, owing to the political dilemma affecting his family, were those that provided Robert Boyle with extra motives for greater concentration on his own interests.

In an age when marriage was often arranged in early youth, Robert had escaped, even though the Earl of Cork had already given a ring on Robert's behalf, when he was only thirteen, to Ann Howard, daughter of Lord Edward Howard of Escrick. There was also a bequest in the Earl's Will of a Silver Cistern, a Silver Kettle and a Silver Ladle, which had cost £274 18s.6d. to the lady should she be married to his son, Robert, on the Earl's decease. This did not take place as the Earl had hoped. Ann married her cousin, Charles Howard, in 1645, and Robert dedicated his life to his work.

It was in his Stalbridge Manor House that Robert Boyle showed great concern for the setting up of the furnace in his first laboratory and it was there that he began his experiments and writings that later brought him international fame. By the end of 1646 the new Lord of the Manor had been impatient to install a laboratory in his Stalbridge home, but the first furnace arrived, having travelled a thousand miles, crumbled in pieces, and it was not until 1649 that he was able to write to his sister Katherine, that,

'Vulcan has so transformed and bewitched me to make me fancy my laboratory as a kind of Elizium.'

That he was not unaware of estate management is shown in a letter Boyle wrote to Benjamin Worsley, dated by Maddison to be shortly after November 21st, 1646, in which he stated

'My grand employment, in my spare hours, is to catechise my gardener and our ploughmen concerning the fundamentals of their profession.'

Robert Boyle used his house to receive visitors, as well as making it a retreat in which he could follow his own interests, – albeit rather empty after the family gatherings he had known before his travels abroad, and sadly described by him on his return as 'my own ruined cottage in the country', is known from his own letters.

Boyle was also writing prodigiously on all manner of subjects. Although his scientific interests had been stimulated by meetings in London of the Philosophical

College from 1645 onwards, and by his friends whom he styled the 'Invisible' College, the scientific content of Robert's writings at this time was less than a third of his total output.

His essays also included moral, ethical and philosophical subjects. Following affirmations of faith during a thunderstorm whilst in Geneva, his studies were guided by firm moral and religious principles, and supported by his stay in London with his sister and her in-laws.

One of his early works, completed before he left Stalbridge in 1655, was *The Martyrdom of Theodora and Didymus*, which Dr Johnson acknowledged to be the first religious romance. Handel's oratorio, 'Theodora', produced in London a century later, from which comes the well-known aria, 'Angels ever bright and fair', was based on Boyle's book.

Another of his works, entitled *Occasional Reflections upon Several Subjects*, and not published until 1665, was begun in Stalbridge and touched upon rural life, horseshoes, and boys swimming with air bladders. It also questioned standards of judgement, asking why people in other nations were despised for eating caterpillars etc, when hundreds of mites, "really crawling insects bred out of putrefactions," were devoured and swallowed alive in the eating of the Dorset blue-veined cheese.

The book aroused Swift to a satirical response entitled, *A Pious Meditation upon a Broomstick, in the Style of the Honourable Mr. Boyle.*

Some sources suggest that Robert suffered ill health from boyhood, and while he was living in Stalbridge he was prescribed treatment for the stone, evidently suffering from the age of 21 from a 'torturing malady'. It was generally believed that he would take the temperature of the air before choosing from his "divers sorts of cloaks" for his outings from his Stalbridge House.

An indenture, dated 1648, between Robert Boyle and Hugh Watts of Stalbridge, concerning 23 acres of closes and parcels of meadow known as Winterhedges in STALBRIDGE cost Hugh Watts £315, but he had to allow Robert Boyle the privilege to 'hawk and hunt' at 'convenient and seasonable times'. It would be interesting to know whether the Lord of the Manor ever took advantage of the sport.

One of Boyle's letters, written from Stalbridge in August 1649, is printed here to show something of the nature of the man and the strict regime that he kept with regard to work. He had, by this time, received his new furnace, which elicits the most joyful tone in the letter, regretting sadly the visits and time wasting of well-wishers after his illness.

My sister
    I must confesse that I shud be as much in your debt for Letters, tho I had answer'd every one of yours; as he is in his Creditor's asks for two Angells has payd backe but two Shillings.
    . . . I am heere, God bee prays'd, upon the mending hand: tho not yet exempted either from Payne or Feare; the latter of which I could wish (but believe not) as

Above This view of the High Street in about 1860 is one of the earliest known photographs to be taken in Dorset, and was probably taken at the same time as the photograph on the front cover.

Right Silk Hay, at the junction of the High Street and Silk House Barton, was formerly part of a substantial medieval merchant's house.

Two views of Ring Street.
Above Looking south from the village centre in the early 20th century. The first cottage on the right has since been demolished.
Below Looking north in the 1930s. The warehouse on the right and the last cottage on the left have both been demolished.

Two views of Church Hill in the early 20th century. The wall in the upper photograph was erected following the demolition of two cottages there. Later this became the site of Lovelace's Garage and showroom. The wall there today dates from 1964. The pub on the right in the lower photograph was the Red Lion, which was de-licensed in 1961.

Stalbridge Cross in about 1920. The 15th century Market Cross is built of limestone from Marnhull or Todber and is the best-preserved in Dorset.

Above An 1838 pen and wash sketch by an unknown artist of the Church of St Mary, Stalbridge, as it looked in the late 18th century – prior to the Victorian alterations.

Below Stalbridge Church, the nave.

Above Stalbridge Church. A 15th or 16th century table tomb with a life-size cadaver effigy. The tomb has a marked similarity to the nearby Thornhill table tomb.

Left Stalbridge Church. The Memorial to Rector William Douch, 1648, and Joanna, 'his wife and a pious matron', 1667. William Douch was Robert Boyle's tutor. The two round-headed panels are linked by clasped hands.

Above Stalbridge Church. A stone carving said to be by Thornhill of his patron George II on the capital of one of the columns in the Weston Chapel.

Below Stalbridge Church, 13th century font on modern plinth.

Left The scientist Robert Boyle (1627-1691). Boyle was one of the founders of the Royal Society, and is today best-remembered for the law bearing his name, 'Boyle's Law', which states that the pressure of a gas is in inverse proportion to the volume it occupies.

Opposite page top The Manor of Stalbridge – 'A Goodlie Fair House'. The house, once the fifth largest in Dorset, was demolished in 1822 by the first Marquess of Anglesey, who himself had lost a leg at the Battle of Waterloo.

Opposite page bottom The 17th century gate piers at the entrance to Stalbridge Park. The gate piers, park wall, walled kitchen garden and some fragments of stonework in a nearby farmhouse are all that survive of the house today.

Left The author of this book, Irene Jones, beside a replica of the air pump designed by Boyle at the Boyle Exhibition in Sturminster Newton Museum.

Re-enactment in Stalbridge Park of a Civil War battle. Although there was no actual fighting in Stalbridge, Charles I and the Royalist army passed through the town in 1644 and the king spent the night at Stalbridge Park.

The entrance porch to the Nonconformist Meeting House, or Chapel, in Station Road, and later used as a Pump House.

Above An early photograph of Stalbridge Weston, a still unspoilt hamlet on a road leading only to farms. Only the thatch has been replaced.

Below Kingsmill Bridge was built in 1823 by John Stone of Yalcombe to replace a wooden bridge over the River Stour on the road to Marnhull.

Left The artist Sir James Thornhill (1675–1734), from a portrait by Joseph Highmore.

Below The White Hart, Lower Bond Street, Melcombe Regis (Weymouth), Thornhill's birthplace. Thornhill always retained his affection for Melcombe Regis, and from 1722 was one of its two Members of Parliament.

Thornhill House, the east front in 1775. The oriel window was replaced in the 19th century by a two storey porch and the tower has been removed: the bell now hangs in Milton Abbey School. The estate was bought by Thornhill in 1725 and the present house was probably both designed and built by him.

Thornhill House, the south front in 1980.

Above An engraving of Sir James Thornhill's altarpiece of 'The Last Supper' in St Mary's Church, Weymouth.

Left The Thornhill coat-of-arms: 3 blackbirds and a red chevron.

Below A Thornhill table tomb between the chancel and Weston Chapel in Stalbridge Church. Sir James was buried in the church but the precise location is no longer known because of the Victorian alterations.

An engraving of the painted drawing room ceiling at Thornhill House by Sir James Thornhill, with his self-portrait to the left of the centre. Sadly, all the paintings by Thornhill inside the house have disappeared.

An engraving of the obelisk erected in 1727 by Sir James Thornhill to celebrate the accession of his patron, George II, to the throne. It was partly destroyed in a gale in 1836 and rebuilt in its present form by the Rev Henry Boucher in 1874.

The dedication to George II and Queen Caroline on the Thornhill Obelisk.

IN HON. DOM. AVGVSTAE
V. ID. OCTOB. CIƆDCCXXVII
DIE INAVGVRANDIS SS. PP.
GEORGIO II: ET CAROLINAE
MAG. BRITAN FRAN. ET HIBERN.
R. ET R. SOLENNITER DICATO
IACOBVS THORNHILL EQVES
D. S.   P. C.

much Enemy as to my Reason, as I find the former to my Quiett.

I intend notwithstanding, by God's blessing, as soone as I have heere recruited & refresht my Purse and Selfe, to accomplish my Dessein'd Remove to London, my hop't arrivall at which, I looke on with more Joy, as a Fruite of my Recovery than a Testimony of it.

Sr William & his son went hence this Morning, having by the favor (or rather Charity) of a Visit, made mee some Compensation for the many I have lately receiv'd from Persons, whose Visitations (I think I may call them) in spite of my Aversenesse to Physicke, make mee find a greater Trouble in the Congratulations then the Instruments of my Recovery.

You'll pardon, perhaps, the bitternesse of this Expression, when I have told you, that having spent most of this Weeke in drawing (for my particular use) a quintessence of Wormewood, those Disturbers of my Worke, might easily shake some few drops into my Inke.

. . . But my Bloud has soe thicken'd my Inke, that I cannot yet make it runne, any thoughts of Improving the Creatures, have bin very much displac't by those of Leaving them. Nor has my Disease bin more guilty of my Oblivion then my Employment since it has begun to re(?) me.

For Vulcan has so transported and bewitch't mee, that as the Delights I tast in it, make me fancy my Laboratory a kind of Elizium; so as if the Threshold of it possesst the quality the Poets ascribed to that Lethe their Fictions made men taste of before their entrance into those states of Bliss.

I there forget my Standish* and my Bookes and almost all things, but the unchangeable Resolution I have made of (?) till Death.

Sister Yours

R. B.

[* Writing Stand]

It is obvious from the letter that Boyle cherished the visits of people like William Petty but hated distractions from his work and scientific investigations.

One of Boyle's Dorset friends, whose visits must have been of reciprocal stimulus and benefit, was Nathaniel Highmore, who practised medicine in Sherborne. His father had been Rector of Purse Caundle, and perhaps because of this, Nathaniel evidently never took a fee from the clergy.

It is clear from the dedication to Robert Boyle in Highmore's book entitled *The History of Generation* in 1651, that Highmore was well acquainted with the young writer:

'You have, Sir, so inricht your tender years with such choice principles of the best sorts . . . that you stand both a pattern and a wonder to our Nobility and gentry . . . you have not thought your blood and descent debased, because married to the Arts.'

This shows the respect that Highmore, fourteen years older than Boyle, felt for the younger man, only 24 years old at the time, and also the high regard for his output of work and thought.

Highmore's publications, which included several medical books, one on 'Human Anatomy', which was unfinished, and a *Discourse of the Cure of Wounds by Sympathy,* and books on hysterics and hypochondria, provide some indication of the influence that Highmore might have given to the direction of Boyle's medical enquiries.

Having an aversion to physic from an early age, Robert was alerted to the effects of prescriptions while a young boy at Eton; he having been given a syrup of stewed prunes by the maids when he did not like taking the physician's purge prescribed for the ague. Robert had been most amused at the doctor's keen desire to ascribe the recovery to the 'efficacy of the potion'.

Even then, the boy perceptively discerned that the ague may have disappeared through the natural course of events, or that his mirth in deceiving the doctor may have helped the cure.

Observations in a letter of 1646 suggest that soon after his arrival in Stalbridge, Boyle was interested in experiments and probably those 'having a bearing on medicinal curative value.' By 1650, his essays included:

Some Assumptions about Destillation examin'd;
Of the Efficacy of vnpromising Medecines;
Of the Effluvia & Pores of Bodys.

Extracts from two later letters show the interest that Highmore created; one letter from Sir William Petty, with whom Boyle studied the circulation of the blood in Ireland, and the other, written by Boyle, confirm that Highmore actually visited him in Stalbridge Park.

Dr (afterwards Sir William) Petty to the hon. Mr Boyle.
'Dublin, April 15, 1653.
My cousin Highmore's curious hand hath shewn you so much of the fabric of man's body, that you cannot think but that so complete a piece of yourself will be always at some little fault or other.'

Mr Boyle to Mr Oldenburg.
'Oxford, Aug 29, 1664.
I was visited in Dorsetshire by the ingenious Dr. Highmore, from whom I had some odd anatomical observations, wherewith I may hereafter acquaint you. I shall rather tell you now, that he is a great florist; and finds, by experience, that there is scarce any mold comparable for flowers to the earth which is digged from under old stacks of wood, or other places where rotten wood has long lain.'

Highmore also carried out some analysis of spring and spa waters and his *Account of the springs at Farringdon and East Chinnock in Dorset* and *Considerations on Scarborough Spa* were published in the Philosophical Transactions of the Royal Society.

He distinguished himself by discovering a new duct in the testicles, and from him the antrum Highmorianum, or great cavity in the jaw, took its name. His twenty-one plates of anatomical figures were given to the Royal Society. He died in 1685/6, aged 71 and was buried in Purse Caundle Church.

Robert Boyle's name appeared in the Dorset Hearth Tax Returns of 1662-1664, when Stalbridge House, with its numerous rooms, was assessed for 30 hearths, 1 missing, but he was no longer resident in the House.

No doubt feeling himself in rural isolation in his Stalbridge laboratory, in 1655/6, Robert took lodgings in Oxford, where he had found "a knot of such ingenious and free philosophers who do not only admit and entertain real learning but cherish and improve it." In High Street, Oxford, he set up his laboratory and engaged Robert Hooke as his assistant.

His book, *The Sceptical Chymist*, was published in 1661, and in it, through experiments of his own, some perhaps begun in Stalbridge, observed painstakingly, for as long as five years, he set out to query the fundamental philosophical notions of the alchemists, who continued to believe in the four elements of the Aristotelians.

Experimental data, which confirmed his hypothesis 'that pressures and volume were in reciprocal proportion', known as 'Boyle's Law', relating to perfect gases, studied later by countless generations of schoolchildren, appeared during his residence in Oxford in 1662, as an appendage to the second edition of his work entitled, 'New Experiments Physico-Mechanical touching the Spring of the Air and its Effects, made, for the most part, in a new Pneumatical Engine'.

On the Restoration of the Monarchy in 1660, Boyle deemed it necessary to obtain the pardon of the King, Charles II.

This he signed on 5th June 1660, declaring that he, Robert Boyle of Stalbridge would remain His Majesty's loyal and obedient servant.

THE KING'S PARDON

In pursuance of the gratious declaration of his most excellent matie, and my soveraigne lord Charles the Second, by the grace of God, King of England, Scotland, France, and Ireland, Defender of the Faith, given under his matie's syne mannuell and privy signet at court, at Breda, the 14th of Aprill last, and upon the first of May last ordered by the commons house to be printed and published.

I Robert Boyle, of Stalbridge, esq. doe with thankfullness lay hold upon that his matie's said free and generall pardon by the said declaration granted; and I doe publiquely declare, that I doe lay hold upon that his matie's grace and favour; and that I am and will continue his matie's loyall and obedient subject. In testimony whereof, I have hereunto subscribed my name this fifth day of June, in the twelveth yeare of his matie's raigne, one thousand six hundred and sixty.

ROBERT BOYLE.

This declaration was published, made and subscribed the same fifth day of June 1660, by the said Robert Boyle, before me,

HAR. GRIMSTON, Speaker of the House of Commons.'

The same year saw also the beginnings of the Royal Society meeting in Gresham College, which was formed 'for improving all useful sciences, arts and inventions by experiments'.

Robert Boyle was much involved, and his name was on the First Charter granted in 1662. He presented his nine experiments before King Charles, who showed a great interest in the Society's activities. Boyle presented his first air pump to the Royal Society in 1661 and many experiments were performed before visitors, it being one of the Society's first show pieces.

In 1668 Boyle left Oxford to spend the rest of his life in London, preferring to live in London with his sister, Katherine, in a house in Pall Mall, where, according to Aubrey, he had a 'noble laboratory' and several apprentices.

His researches for the Royal Society were prolific, and his numerous books and pamphlets included work on heat, colours, optics, a graduated thermometer and electricity.

Boyle also pioneered the translation of the Bible into several languages, and it was through his agency that the Society for the Propagation of the Gospel was founded. He did not take orders, believing that he could better further the cause of the church from outside the profession. He refused the Provostship of Eton and would not accept his election as President of the Royal Society, because of his sensitivity towards the taking of Oaths. In London, as in Oxford, he was in touch with the foremost thinkers of the age, and welcomed visitors from abroad, always anxious to learn of the latest scientific ideas and research.

Robert Boyle remained Lord of the Manor of Stalbridge until he died on 30th December 1691, only one week after his sister, Katherine. He was buried at his own request, without ostentation, the cost not to exceed £250, next to Katherine, in the Chancel of St. Martin-in-the-Fields.

His friend Dr. Burnet, Bishop of Salisbury, delivered the funeral oration, reported at length in the diary of John Evelyn, who concluded,

"And truly all this was but his due,
and without any grain of flattery."

As the Church of St. Martin-in-the-Fields was rebuilt in the 1720's, and bones later removed, there is no memorial of Boyle's last resting-place.

ROBERT BOYLE'S WILL

Many people may wonder why Stalbridge has no memorial to Robert Boyle, although he was Lord of the Manor for close on fifty years, when Yetminster possesses a building, known as Boyle's School, which was established some years after his death in 1691, by John Warr, one of his executors, with money from the estate.

Boyle certainly retained affection for Stalbridge although he had lived his later life in Oxford and London. He styled himself in his Will as "Robert Boyle of Stalbridge, and left bequests of plate to the value of ten pounds to John Nicholls, "faithfull friend . . . Gent & Steward" of the Courts of the Manor of Stalbridge, and to Nicholas Watts, Bailiff of the Manor of Stalbridge.

He also remembered his tenants in Stalbridge, specifying that charges for legal engagements with them should be concluded, and he pledged a distribution of money to the poor of the parish of Stalbridge.

The bequest of his best watch to his brother Francis, was to remind him of the expense of keeping up the Manor House of Stalbridge without "intending to live in it for his sake." As Boyle never married, his entailed lands, including the

Stalbridge estate, returned to his eldest brother, Richard, Earl of Burlington.

The Boyle Lectures, begun soon after his death, "against Atheists, Deists, Libertines, Jews," were presented annually, but payments were not made until 1697 when the three executors of the Will were brought to Court for their tardiness in making provision for the £50 fee to the lecturers.

The Chancery Decree also approved the proposals for the disposal of the residue of Boyle's estate, which consisted of charitable bequests, one of which, put forward by John Warr, one of the three executors, was the establishment of a Charity School.

John Warr, Boyle's servant, had become Boyle's executor, replacing Katherine, Boyle's sister, following her death only one week before the demise of Boyle himself. By 1699, Warr had acquired 40 acres of land in Knighton, Beer Hacket, Dorset, and the income supported the school-house and school built at Yetminster for 20 poor boys from Yetminster, Chetnole and Leigh, 'to be taught reading, writing and arithmetic, so as to qualify them to be put out as apprentices.' The first master was George Rawles. John Warr died in 1715.

Boyle's School was absorbed by Yetminster County School in 1947, and the endowment, known as Boyle's Educational Foundation, still operates through its Trustees, with funds available for Yetminster, Chetnole and Leigh applicants, and other educational projects in the village of Yetminster.

A portrait of Robert Boyle, a replica of the painting by Kerseboom, circa 1689, that once hung in the school-house, is now in the Dorset County Museum.

Boyle gave some of his books to the free Grammar School in Sherborne and these are held in the collection of Antiquarian books in the library of Sherborne School.

Apart from the distinctive seventeenth century lion-crested terminals, on the massive gate piers guarding the entrance to Stalbridge Park, nothing of the huge manor house, where Boyle began his writing and experiments that gave him an international reputation in his life-time, remains except the bare site mounds and the walled garden.

Nothing has so far come to light to show that Boyle had any direct connections with Yetminster, and one must assume that the school was built there through John Warr's interests, financial or otherwise. Yetminster retains the building, now a private residence, adorned by the blue and white plaque stating that it was the original Boyle's School.

It is unfortunate that Stalbridge, which Boyle had known through several years' residence in the first half of his life, should have nothing tangible to remind the world of its early influences upon the great 'Father of Chemistry'.

THIRTEEN

Stuart Stalbridge

There is little available documentation of the early seventeenth century history of Stalbridge to reflect national events such as the ending of the reign of Elizabeth, and the reception of the new Scottish King, James I. Nor can we learn whether the first of the century's three Bubonic plagues, raging in London in 1603 as the King was making his way to Whitehall, was also affecting the rural areas, there being no parish register of this period in which to check untoward occurrences.

News of the Gunpowder Plot, which tried to blow up King and Parliament in 1605, following soon afterwards, no doubt eventually reached Dorset, but the disturbances in Stalbridge in the early seventeenth century appear to have been domestic rather than political. From the entries in the first Churchwardens' Account Book, 1694-1761, Stalbridge did remember the 5th November, – it was the birthday of King William III – but it was also remembered as Gunpowder, Treason Day, with a peal of bells, if not other, more active, celebrations.

Some of the inhabitants had their own private quarrels at the beginning of the century and it is from the records of the legal disputes that we can gather a few facts about the town itself.

It must have relied heavily upon agriculture at this time, but from occupations of witnesses at the legal trials, it is possible to gain some idea of the ways in which more commercial aspects of life were taking hold.

From suits at law, we can also learn of the problems and attitudes of the people, as well as names and ages of witnesses. It appears that the Stalbridge community was quite vociferous, not only against the will of the Earl of Castlehaven in 1618 when he wished to build the new Manor House and enclose the ground around it, but also in the number of private cases involving disputes over Wills and arguments about property and animals.

The extracts are taken from *Dorset Depositions* by Pope and unless stated otherwise, the names given are of persons from Stalbridge.

SOME STALBRIDGE RESIDENTS 1600-1659

1618 BISHOPP v MORLEY

Alan Bishopp, clerk, aged 34, had been kept out of his church and living at Stalbridge by Defendant Caleb Morley, clerk, by means of manifold suits at law by the said Caleb, Thomas Morley and Gabriel Puckle and is fallen into such poverty that he is not worth in money or goods £5.

According to the list of Stalbridge Incumbents, Alan Bishop, was Rector, 1609 - 1615 and Caleb Morley, Rector, 1615 - 1621

1621 CAULPYN v LAWRENCE

Gabriell Caulpyn, broad weaver, married to Elizabeth Bugge, daughter of Thomas Bugge of Okeford Fitzpaine, freemason, who died when aged, feeble and blind, leaving his young second wife as executrix. She married John Lawrence, who 'confederated' with Nicholas Romminge, yeoman, of Lidlinch, and Robert Bugge to suppress the Will leaving money to the children of Bugge's first marriage.

1626 Will of WILLIAM WATTS

Defendant Elizabeth Gray, daughter of William Watts. William Watts of Stalbridge Weston, yeoman, died possessed of copyhold in Stalbridge Weston, part called Hewpitt alias Steenford (steen = O.E. stone, cf Harpitts later and quarrying, 1837), and of kyne and sheep, all valued at £400.

Executors: Elnathan Atkins; Faith Atkins, married to Anthony Davidge: Suzan Atkins, married to Thomas Senyor.

1635 at Shaston
RICHARD MAWDESLEY, gen. aged 38

1636 FILL v LAWRENCE and AVICE COMBE, EDWARD COMBE, JOHN HILSDON, alias BURGE, the elder, JOHN HILSDON, alias BURGE, the younger, MATTHEW HILSDON, alias Burge, WILLIAM WHITE & . . . KEYNELL.

Nicholas Fill of Lidlinch, Purveyor to His Majesty for 'Beefs, Muttons & lambes' in the County of Dorset, had agreed with Lawrence and Avice Combe for the pasturing of cattle on lands called Remples in Stalbridge containing 75 acres at £45 a year.

Plaintiff's cattle forcibly driven out, impounded, and bruised by Defendants. Injunction granted to restrain Defendants.

1637 NICHOLAS FILL of Lidlinch, gen., sued LAWRENCE COOMBE of Stalbridge, and EDWARD COOMBE of Tisbury, yeoman.

John Gally, gen, aged 35
William Jeanes, husbandman, aged 54
Anthony Browne, yeoman, aged 50
Maurice Langhorne, clerk, aged 38
William Gill, husbandman, aged 40
Richard Mandesley, gen aged 40

1639 WILLOUGHBY v ANCKETILL at Stalbridge

John Willoughby, gen., Richard Bragg, gen., George Snooke, Joseph Loder, Michael Watts and John Galpin v Francis Ancketill.

Sir Ferdinando Tutchett, Knt deceased, bequeathed £100 in his will to the poor of Stalbridge. He had lived with his brother the Earl of Castlehaven at Stalbridge and received part of his education in the town.

John Jeanes, tayler, aged 46, had been a scholler with Tutchett in the town of Stalbridge.

The suit concerned the bequest and an alleged intention on the part of the testator to give either land or money in his lifetime to the use of four poor aged men of Stalbridge.

John Jenys, of Sterte, gen aged 61, plaintiff Willoughby, Richard Mandesley, gen., were all chief residents of Stalbridge

Others mentioned – Frances Bottom, widow, aged 70, Stephen Gawtrell, barber, aged 53, Oliver Symes, John Jenys of Sterte, Dorset, gen., aged 61.

1640 LAWRENCE COMBE v JOHN HILSDON alias BURGE
Concerning lands called Rymples in Stalbridge

1650 At Wincanton
ANN SIMES, widow, aged 60. ELNATHAN ATKINS, gen. aged 44.

1651 Plaintiff, JOHN PAWLETT.
Katherine Pawlett wished to live apart from her husband, John Pawlett of Holdinesse, Dorset, who deposited £740 for her benefit in the hands of her sister, Ellinor Hill, widow, of Stalbridge.

Ellinor Hill had purchased a lease of land at Weston from George Thornhull Esq.

1656 John THORNEHILL, gen, v Hugh COXSHED, yeoman, of Thornehill in Stalbridge. Dispute over property and 24 acres of land in Stalbridge.

1659? Bonds: -
JOHN CREW of Stalbridge Weston, husbandman, aged 72
GRACE LONGE of Frythe House, Stalbridge, widow, aged 64
JOAN ELLIS, wife of Hugh Ellis, Stalbridge, woollen weaver, aged 30
HUGH WESTON, (the younger), of Frythe House, Stalbridge, gent, aged 29

From the legal suit, FILL v COMBE, 1636 above, we find that land in Stalbridge was being used to graze cattle, possibly for King Charles I, through Nicholas Fill, of Lydlinch, who rented land at 'Remples' for the pasturing of cattle – 75 acres at £45 a year.

The sale of beef for tables outside Stalbridge may have been arranged through Stalbridge market; there is no other hint of the continuance of a market during the whole of this century.

From the suit concerning the will of Ferdinando Touchet, brother of Mervyn, Earl of Castlehaven, it is evident that there was a school in Stalbridge for John

Jenys had been a 'scholar' at the school in the town with Ferdinando.

The money bequeathed by Ferdinando Touchet became known as Ferdinando's Charity and there are records of its distribution to the poor of Stalbridge during the eighteenth century.

THE TRIAL OF MERVYN, EARL OF CASTLEHAVEN

The Trial of Mervyn, Earl of Castlehaven, in 1631, in London, followed by his execution, cannot have gone unnoticed by the inhabitants of Stalbridge, several of whom were no doubt employed by him in Stalbridge House and Park, for he was at some time resident in Stalbridge, at least one of his children having been born in Stalbridge.

THE GREAT EARL OF CORK AT STALBRIDGE

The refurbishment of Stalbridge House from 1636 by the 'great' Earl of Cork brought in specialist masons and plumbers from outside the small market town, but local labour must have been drafted in for drawing the stone from the Stalbridge and Marnhull quarries and for the less specialised work.

The fact that the Earl of Cork kept his garden locked, – in 1639 bestowing the key upon his youngest son, Robert, as a great favour, – was a means of protecting his 'bon chritons & burgoynes', the new pears he had planted, and other unusual fruits and vegetables, perhaps a great innovation to the palates of Stalbridge.

The arrival of the army from Ireland, en route for the King's Scottish Expedition in 1639 with the Earl's sons, must have fluttered many a native girl's heart as well as depleting the supply of fowls and other meats in the neighbourhood.

Only five years later, Stalbridge was subject again to an 'invasion' when the impact of Charles I and his army in 1644 must also have been impressed upon many, by the imposition, if not the insistence, on the generosity of local hearths.

PROTESTATION OATH

During the period of unease before the outbreak of the Civil War, Parliament had organised a signed protest against the possibility of 'an arbitrary and tyranical government'. The form of protestation that each individual had to sign is given here, followed by the long list of 244 men of Stalbridge who promised, vowed and protested. Only one man did not sign. The list of men from all four Stalbridge tithings was headed by the Rev. Willliam Douch, who administered the Oath. He had been tutor to Robert Boyle in 1638.

I doe, in the presence of Almightie God, promise, vow, and protest to maintaine and defend, so farre as lawfullie I may, with my life, power, and estate, the true Reformed

Protestation Religion expressed in the doctrine of the Church of England, against all Poperie and Popish Innovations within this Realme contrarie to the same Doctrine and according to the dutie of my Allegiance to his Ma'ties Royall person, honor, and estate.

The Justices of the Peace in the Sherborne division were Wm Coke and John Walcot.

PROTESTATION RETURNS FOR STALBRIDGE 1641/2

William Douch Rector	George Rabbetts	John Foote, ju	
Gabriell Basley	John Snooke	Thomas Weston Esqr	Thomas Drew ju.
William Foote	William Weston gent	William Turner	Thomas Pownall
James Weston gent	Michaell Snooke sen	Peter Cole	Robt Colborne
Christopher Jeanes	Thomas Dike	Thomas Nayler	John Crew
Anthoney Browne	Robert Moore	John Gerrard	Robt Browne
Richard Bragg	John Rabbetts	Giles Douch	Christopher Batt
John Cryar	William Allens	Steven Gautrill	Thomas Locket
Osmund Hunt	John King	William Sage	Edward Dober
Thomas Snooke	John Browne	William Dober	Thomas Ridout
Walter Stone	John Symes	George Ridout	Thomas Foote
Nicholas Actwell	William Signior	Arthur Miles	Thomas Snooke
Richard Snooke	Thomas Bastable	James Bishopp	John Savage
William Ridout	Roger Greene	Osmund Plant	Edward Locke
Thomas Turner	Robt Turner	Richard Hutchins	John Jeanes
William Pitman	Walter Scott	John Hunt	Michaell Snooke
Hugh Lymmen	Thomas Locke	Thomas Drew sen	George Duffett
William Hunt	Robt Lymmen	William Buffett	Robt Tyte
Nicholas Hutchins	John Hopkins	William Chamberlaine	John Snooke
John Foote sen	George Younge	Thomas Marks	James Gosse
Thomas Lymmen	William Tooke	Henry Babstocke	Edward Kenison
Thomas Ellis	Nicholas Symes	Richard Pinn	Thomas Snooke
Bernard Poole	John Lambert	Roger May	Thomas Snooke
Peter Fudge	John Scott	George Chamberlaine	Walter Sandale
George Babstocke	Robert Kellaway	Stokes Allin	William Gill
William Poole	Hugh Ellis	Thomas Murrey	Bartholomew Randall
George Stone	William Browne	Frauncis Bleeke	John Champion
Bernard Jeanes	John Chamberlaine	Frauncis Buffett	John Walter
Thomas Fudge	George Browne	Richard Walter	John Loader
Thomas Duffett	Joseph Loader	William Locke	William Coombe
William Cutler	George Wilton	James Fyander	John Snooke
William Duffett	Sidracke Phelpes	Laurence Browne	Elnathan Jeanes
Thomas Gautrill	Robt Signior	John Ginkin	Philipp Cuffe
Henry Snooke	William Jeanes	Henry Duffett	Gabriell Calpin
Richard Tickrill	Michael Snooke sen	John Bastable	James Cuffe
Thomas Bastable	William Kimber	Nicholas Signior	Thomas Watts
William Bennett	Christopher Snooke	Symon Haine	John Ridout
James Jeanes	Richard Snooke	William Douch	Martin Colborne

Benjamin King
William Everett
William Buffett
John Gray
George Snooke
Robert Kimber
Walter Buckler
Bernard Jeanes
Thomas Vowles
Ambrose Browne
Robert Jeloff sen
Robert Poole
John Arney
John Calpin
William Tucker
William Barton
John Bastable
William Locke
Thomas Cole
Hugh Snooke
Robert Tyte
William Kember
Robert Bastable
Richard Snooke

Steven Savage
James Mitchell
William Loader
William Purdue
Robert Jeloffe sen
John Carter
William Stone
William Hulett
George Lockett
John Hunt
Richard Symes
Hosea Poole
Robert Coombe
Richard Davyes
Thomas Snooke
Thomas Pope
John Browne
Hugh Lymmen
Thomas Farvis
James Poole
Edward White
William Duffett
William Scutt

Robt Burleton
John Duffett
Thomas Bastable
Richard Chamberlaine
John Segar
Leonard Helliar
Thomas Hann
Thomas Vine
Henry Lockett
Robert Longman
John Browne
Henry Ferrard
William Maudesley
Thomas Locke
John Percie
Thomas Hann
Richard Burleton
Willm Champion
Mathew Duffett
Mathew Pinn
John Jeanes
William Watts
Hugh Weston gent

Michaell Watts
Thomas Jeanes
John Snooke
George Brine
John Townsend
George Russell
Walter Stone
William Pavett
George Green
William Chamberlaine
Lawrence Poole
John Drew
William Calpin
John Markes
William Worthington
Richard Browne
Robert Hobbs
William Burt
William Scott
William Tyte
William Jeanes
Nathaniell Kember
George Lymmen

George Barnard hath not protested.
All they whoses names are before written have willingly protested before mee,
Will. Douch, rector of Stalbridge.
John Locke x constable Willm Pavet x churchwarden

    Henry Townsend x churchwarden
      Hugh Watts   )
      John Calpin   ) overseers of
      William Chamberlen) the poore.

FOURTEEN

The Civil War in North Dorset

By the time Robert Boyle, the new Lord of the Manor arrived in Stalbridge around the end of 1644, the northern part of the county of Dorset had already experienced some of the turmoil and strife of the Civil War.

Several incidents had shattered the peace of the towns in 1643 and the various contingents of armies marching through the villages could not have left even the smaller hamlets untouched. Details of the marches, pillaging and skirmishes were recorded by Hutchins in his *History of Dorset*.

There is no evidence of damage by the Parliamentarians in Stalbridge Church, as in Sherborne, Sydling, Wimborne and Gillingham; the unfortunate loss of the Parish Register, vital for this period, does not allow us to judge any isolated incidents such as the deaths of soldiers in the area.

In 1643 there had been a public parade of Lady Arundel and her children through Shaftesbury after Wardour Castle was taken, and the five cartloads of furniture and hangings removed to Dorchester. Fat cattle were driven away to Lyme, Poole and Wareham to feed the garrisons.

The town of Sherborne had been pillaged in April 1643, by Parliamentary troops, when houses were burnt, fat sheep and calves killed and almost all the barley and malt in the town taken away.

In Blandford in the same year, Sir William Waller and his soldiers stayed in the town, levying the sum of £500. The arrival of the opposing Royalists later disturbed the inhabitants in another demand for fees and quarters. Blandford was under assault yet again in June 1644, when Essex's army marched through, and in July, the town was visited and plundered by Major Sydenham and others.

Although Stalbridge was not directly involved in any reported outburst of fighting, or plunder, King Charles was drawn into the south west in the autumn of 1644, and his journey across Dorset, brought the King and his army into the midst of the town in October 1644.

Marching from the south west, Symonds's Diary records

'1 October Mon. King left Chard, kept the road, dyned at Lord Paulet's, and that night to South Porret, first parish in Dorsetshire.'

At Maiden Newton, it is stated that

'Oct 1 1644 King Charles I at Mr Osborne's, had his dinner in the field.'

One can imagine the consternation of the Dorset villagers with troops moving as if preparing for confrontation.

'Tues. 2nd Oct. 1644. Most of this day was spent at the generall rendezvous on Newton Downe, near where the King lay being Mayden Newton. The troope at Kingcombe. This day Prince Rupert came to his Majestie from Bristoll.'

(The day and date is somewhat confusing here as 30th September 1644, fell on a Monday.)

Later that day, the Royalists arrived in Sherborne, and the King was entertained by Lord Digby, dining in the field at Sherborne Lodge.

For Tuesday, 8th October 1644, Symonds' wrote

' . . . the King marched from Sherborne and lay that night at Stawbridge, the faire house of the Earl of Corke . . . the north yle of this church is full of old coates. Wee returned to our quarters.'

Stalbridge, like the other places en route, must have shared the excitement and anticipation of the arrival of the King's army, but cannot have remained unscathed after the intrusion of such an army into the small town, requiring all the food, sustenance and other entertainment that could be mustered before departure next day.

From Stalbridge, the army marched to Sturminster Newton, where on

'. . . October 9. Ch. I dined in the field at Mr Reeve's.

(There is a tradition that His Majesty was sumptuously regaled with green pease for dinner – hence the field name – Pease lease.)

The King's route was along the Stour valley to Durweston, where the King stayed at Bryanston and on Sunday, 13th October, read a lesson in Blandford Church. From thence he marched to Cranborne, evidently without opposition.

'1644 Monday, October 14. This day His Majestie marched before ye foot on foot. His Majestie left Brainston (Bryanston) & wth his whole army marched that night over downs to Cranborn & lay in a faire stone house of the Earl of Salisbury'.

The rising of the Clubmen in 1645 showed the disinclination to take part in civil battle of a large number of men, especially land workers, who merely wished to farm in peace. Many places such as Blandford and Sherborne had suffered from visits of both armies in the Civil War, the towns of Dorset being the strategic targets chosen by the Parliamentarians.

Shaftesbury and Gillingham were subdued by the presence of Waller, who quartered his men in both towns. At some period, the organ in Gillingham church was demolished by Waller's soldiers, and they also plundered Edward Davenant's house; his library, worth £1000, was seized by Waller's soldiers, but later redeemed.

The burials of two Parliamentarian soldiers at Folke on 22nd and 24th July, 1645, one slain in the court and one at Alweston, together with reputed battle scars around the doorway of West Hall, give further evidence of skirmishes in several parts of Dorset, and not only in the larger towns.

The action became increasingly closer to Stalbridge on the southern side, for on 3rd July 1645, Clubmen of Dorset and Wilts were reported to have forced the Parliament quarters in Sturminster Newton. Several men were killed on both sides but 16 dragoons, horses and arms were taken by the Clubmen, providing them with confidence for the coming onslaught with Cromwell.

The Clubmen were alarmed enough to try to stop the slaughter which was taking place throughout the countryside by the continual attacks from both sides and only desired to be able to carry on their lives normally. Amongst the men rallying to the call were John Pope of Marnhull and John Phill, 'a grasier of Lidlinch', but none named from Stalbridge.

On August 2nd, the Clubmen met in Shaftesbury; fifty of their leaders were seized and sent to London, the rest having been dispersed by Colonel Fleetwood.

Determined to make a stand, on 4th August, 4,000 of the Clubmen assembled on Hambledon Hill, and Cromwell was forced to march out of Sherborne to quell the land workers' protest. With experienced troops against them, the Clubmen did not hold out long and suffered defeat, many escaping by sliding down the steep sides of the hill. Cromwell locked up 400 prisoners in Child Okeford Church. His troops were then quartered in Shroton.

Returning to Sherborne through the countryside of North Dorset, Cromwell was heavily occupied in breaking down the defences of Sherborne Castle, the home of the Digby family. Unable to penetrate the castle by assault and battery above, Cromwell had to bring in miners from the Mendips to undermine the foundations. The siege lasted 16 days before the ancient walls gave way to the invaders and Sherborne was subdued.

Stalbridge does not appear to have been involved in any of the skirmishes, possibly because of its geographical situation, just south of the main highway, Sherborne to Shaftesbury and London, and north of the route, Sherborne to Sturminster and Blandford.

During 1645, many Dorset estates were sequestered, those closest to Stalbridge being Bagber, Fifehead Neville, Sturminster Newton, Hinton St. Mary, Margaret Marsh, Motcombe, Gillingham, East Stour, Stour Provost, Marnhull, Purse Caundle, Pulham, Middlemarsh, Hermitage and Long Burton.

The section on Robert Boyle and his connections gives reasons why he may have avoided losing his Stalbridge Estate, or compounding for a great sum, despite his father's support of the King and the King's visit to Stalbridge in 1644.

Although remote, the isolated incidents in North Dorset already noted and the following report of one that occurred towards the end of 1645 in Gillingham, must have kept the inhabitants of Stalbridge fearful and alert.

'The first daye of December, Ambrose Lillie, uppon deniall of his horse, was shot to death by a Parliament soldier at his house, and was buried the third day of Dec.'

The only indication of any protest against the authority of the Parliamentarians is given in the Orders of the Dorset Standing Committee when the churchwardens of Stalbridge had failed to pursue the order to collect tithes to pay the 'intruders' who replaced first, the Rev. William Douch, and then his son, Rev. John Douch. William Douch, the younger, was also ordered to collect the tithes of the lands he possessed.

STALBRIDGE PENSIONERS OF THE CIVIL WAR

Amongst the many names in the lists handed to the meetings of the Dorset Quarter Sessions

> 'of all such indigent souldiers as showed themselves loyall and faithfull to his late Matie in the late Warrs and never defected the sayd service . . .'

appear those of several Stalbridge men. Presented by men of substance for each division of Dorset, the men applying for payments or 'pencons' were presumably vetted before names could be accepted.

William ffoote of Stalbridge was listed with several others in 1662, when it was decided

> 'to pay unto each of them the sum of 20s and the Crt will hereafter take it into further consideration so to settle pencons on them according to Demeritts and directed by late Act of Parliament.'

In 1664, there was an order to give Richard Davies of Stalbridge a 'pencon' of 20s and later in the same year, with Thomas Jeanes, Walter Scott, and Thomas Snooke, he was given a payment of 20s for 'necessity and relief'. At a subsequent meeting of the Quarter Sessions, Francis Buffett was given a like payment, and William ffoote a further payment.

There is no indication that the former soldiers were disabled, but it is certain that stories of the Civil War were passed into the folklore of Stalbridge from the participation in this national uprising.

FIFTEEN

Seventeenth Century

NEWNHAM

Newnham, which existed from 1244 as a ring fence farm, (see early Medieval period), was clearly a substantial property in September, 1653, when it was the subject of a sale between Francis Ancketill, son and heir of Francis Anketill, and other gentlemen to one Richard Lanning, the elder, of Pilstreete, Marnhull, for the sum of £160.

The messuage or tenement, known as Numans or Newenhams, with appurtances, lands etc., had belonged to Robert Goldsborough, gent. deceased, and the indenture mentions rights of common and common of pasture, common of Eastovers that he had enjoyed and used. The name Eastovers may refer to the east side of Stalbridge Common, close to where the property was situated, or to Eastover Lane, (variously Eastlip, Eastup) in Stalbridge Weston.

STALBRIDGE TRADE TOKENS

Because of the shortage of coins of the realm and the subsequent suffering of the poor due to the lack of small denominations, a number of traders in several places in Dorset, including Stalbridge, manufactured their own trade tokens during the latter part of the seventeenth century.

Halfpennies and farthings, the lowest denomination of coins ever minted in this country were originally minted of standard silver, but were soon lost and very often clipped, thus reducing the value. Queen Elizabeth had refused to issue what she considered as a debased copper coinage.

Unfortunately, out of many tokens illustrated in Hutchins, Stalbridge was not represented, but details were given of two traders who issued tokens for the use of the people of Stalbridge.

The legend round the coins gave the name, place of residence, date and the sign which indicated a trade or possibly an inn.

The traders were
> Thomas Snooke – A fleur-de-lis
> Of Stalbridge 1658. T.K.S.
> James Cerne – A glove
> Of Stalbridge 1666. J.K.C.

The name of James Cerne does not occur elsewhere in the documents examined for this century, but in the article on Trade Tokens by J.S. Udal, *Proc. D.N.H.& A.S.* Vol IX. the name is given as James Cane. (The name of James Cave, yeoman, was given on a Bond dated 1695.

Thomas Snooke appears in the Dorset Hearth Tax Assessments for 1662/1664 and the wife of one Thomas Snooke, button-maker, was engaged in an adulterous association with Samuel Rich, Rector of Stalbridge in the period following his incumbency which began in 1675.

A further Trade Token of Stalbridge was recorded in Vol XXIX of the Proceedings as belonging to

> Theophilus Collins – 3 cloves
> Of Stalbridge 1669 C TM

There is a record of Temperance Collins, 1666, and her burial stone was recently found in the drain under the church.

Failing more positive identification, there can only be speculation on the meaning of the signs of the trade tokens, during the period when Stalbridge must have been picking up its reputation for hand made silk stockings, woollen weaving and possibly button-making.

DORSET HEARTH TAX 1662-4

The Returns for the Dorset Hearth Tax imposed 1662-4, reveal the size of the imposing mansion with its thirty chimneys that stood in Stalbridge Park, owned, but not at this date occupied by Robert Boyle.

The next house in size in the Stalbridge Tithing was that occupied by Rev. John Douch, which was probably the house later known after the new Rectory was built in 1699 as Vicarage House. This stood on the site on which the National School was built in Duck Lane and was taken down in order that the stone could be used in the building of Thornhill School.

Most houses must have been of modest proportions, probably with no bedroom fireplaces, but there are a few of moderate size with five or six hearths in Weston and Thornhill as well as Stalbridge Tithing.

The fact that Weston had twenty-five dwellings shows that it must have had a considerable population, with as many people as several other small Dorset villages which supported their own churches.

According to Macaulay, the Hearth Tax was disliked by the English because it meant a domiciliary visit for the assessment, and intrusion into the privacy of one's home. The removal of goods, sometimes the vital chattels of the household, or the bed, the poor man's only comfort, in the case of non-payment of tax, caused a lot of distress, with complaints of collectors performing with 'harshness and insolence.'

It was also the subject of verse

> The good old dames, whenever they the chimney men espied,
> Unto their nooks they haste away, their pots and pipkins hide,
> There is not one old dame in ten, and search the nation through,
> But, if you talk of chimney men, will spare a curse or two.

This dreaded tax was removed by William soon after he came to the throne in 1688 after desperate appeals by his new subjects.

STALBRIDGE TITHING

The right honble Robert Boyle Esqr' 30 (1 false returnd)

John Douch Clerke 10	Robert Tite 4	Joseph Harden 2
John Gally 2	Wm Do uch and Tennte 5	Richard Coombe 2
Henry Townsend 2	John Garrett 2	Redigon Sucoke Widd 4
Willm' Pitman 2	Edmond Michell 6	(2 false returnd)
Elnathan Atkins 2	Mrs Bragg Widd 2	Eliz Duffett widd 1
Bernard Seanys 2	Thomas Wattes 5	Mrs Mawdesley wid 3
Robt Townsend 3	Eliza Seanys 6	John Snooke 2
Tho' Rookcliffe 2	Thomas Dyke 2	George Buck 2
John Dussett 1	John Foote senr 3	Thomas Snooke 3

Thomas Snooke for John Haskett 1   Margarett Watts wid' 4

Nichas Burd and Wm Champion 8 1 demoleshd   Widd' Browne 1

Thomas Buck 5 [f.67]	Mabel Burleton widd 3	Mr Watkins 2
Robte Tite in John Gallyes house 3		John Loder 2
James Cave 4	Ben King in Michaell Watts 3	
Mr Hoddinott 3	demoleshd Robte Rumman 2	Willm' Coombe 3
Willm' Cutler 1	Andrew Loder 1	George Browne 2
Mary Hunt widd' 3	Symon Hayne 2	1 false returnd
[f.67d] John King 1	Kathern Snooke widd' 5	Walter Tite 4
Thomas Murry 2	Samuel Boles for Thomas Cooke 3	
Willm' Burdge 3	Stephen Strong 6	
John Hopkins paup 1	Mr Wm' Weston in John Hopkins 3 but 2 et Paup'	
Thomas Lock 2	Wm 'Miles in Wm' Snookes 3	
William Tite 4[f.64d]		

GOMERSHAY TITHING

Mr Robte Stevens 2	John Kenison 2	Laurence Hobbs 4
Mrs Mary Hulett 4	Richard Townesend 2	Mr Titersall 4
Elizab' Tite Widd' 1	Christian Dussett 1	

THORNHILL TITHING

The Lord Sturton 4	Edw Thornhull Esqr' 15	Mr Juce 5
Mr Sacheverill 6	Widd' Capen 3 [f.65]	John Phesant 2
Willm' Persett 4	Willm' Penny 3 1 decayd	Mr Juce 2
Symon Coram 1	Mr Foyle 2	Mr Curry 3
Mr Weston 1	Widd'Scoke 1 Paup'	

WESTON TITHING

Tho'Weston Esqr' 6	Tho'Weston gent' 3	Hugh Weston gent' 4
James Weston gent'	†Richard†	Robert Jollife 3
[f.65d] Mr Pawlett 4	Robte Kimber 2	Robte'Chaffie 2
Richard Snooke 2	John Snooke 1	Robte'Hellyer 2
John Carter 1	Mary Loder 2	Joane Loocke 1

Grace Snooke 2	Margarett Snooke 2	Robte'Hobbes 1
Lawrence Hobbes 1	Bernard Chamberlaine 3	John Snooke 1
Edw'Hellyer 1	Francis Lane 3	John Loder 1
Tho'Stone 1	Widd Stone 2.	

Thornhill House was a considerable size with fifteen hearths, but Weston, home of Thomas Weston Esqr. and possibly the manor house that once stood in the corner of what is now Stalbridge Park, with six chimneys was comparatively modest for a Manor House of the Weston family.

PUNISHMENTS AND PLAGUE

Following the Restoration of Charles II, while the peace of the land was able to accommodate payments to Dorset 'penconers – loyal and faithfull to his late Majesty', it was also necessary to keep the discipline of the majority. Two of the punishments that could be handed out at this time were the burning on the left shoulder or burning of the hand with the letter 'F' (for felon) and the ordering of persons 'to be whipt until the bodies bleede'. Transportation was also a threat.

To prevent the plague spreading throughout the County, on 2nd October, 18 Chas II (1666), an order was made at the Quarter Sessions that there were to be no meetings or assemblies, bear-baiting, bull-baiting, cock-fighting, common plays, entertainments or interludes. This order was to stop people entering from other counties and from travelling about and spreading the plague. Stalbridge, in common with all other places in Dorset, would have had notices published in the market and other 'publick' places.

Although the Manorial Court Rolls for Stalbridge are not in evidence, those for Stalbridge Weston of 1665 and 1666 make no mention of the plague or the restrictions.

SOME STALBRIDGE RESIDENTS 1660 – 1691

Further lists given below show the large numbers of people who were brought into legal disputes. Apart from Wills and Indentures, they also give the only indication of the occupations of Stalbridge's seventeenth century inhabitants.

1668/9 ROBERT & JUDITH FREAKE (possibly not of Stalbridge) sued THOMAS BRANKERE, yeoman, concerning a bond dated at Sherborne 16 Charles 2.

1672 BURT v ROBERT BURLETON
Maintenance of defendant in his minority.
Robert Burleton lived with aunt, Mabel Burt, who then lived with her father, Stephen Gartrell at Stalbridge.
Cicely Gartrell was the widow of Stephen Gartrell of Blandford.
Mabel's son was George Burleton

Christian, wife of Thomas Bastable, aged 63
Joane, wife of Thomas Locke, aged 55
Margery, wife of William Roberts, translator, aged 54
Thomas Willmouth, husbandsman, aged 40
Stephen Strong, husbandsman, aged 39
Elizabeth, wife of Thomas Bastable . . . llier, aged 45

William Combe, victualler;
William Gartrell, barber chyrurgeon, aged 42
This case continued at Stalbridge 21 Jan 1672/3 when the following witnesses were called:
Francis Buffett, woollen weaver, aged 53
Cicely, wife of Phillip Pitman, aged 36
Katherine Bullock, widow, aged 29

(The occupation of translator is a most unusual one to find in Stalbridge unless William Roberts was connected with the legal profession or employed by the occupant of the Manor House.)

(Possibly the missing letters showing the occupation of Thomas Bastable were hellier, or tiler. There were several helliers in the occupations given in the list of baptisms in the Stalbridge Register thirty years later.)

1674 At Wincanton
Elnathan Atkins of Stalbridge, yeoman, aged 56.

OVERCHARGES ON THE POOR RATE

From complaints brought before the Quarter Sessions about being over-rated for the 'Church and the poore', it is clear that in 1665, land in Stalbridge belonged to Richard Newman of Fifehead Magdalen, who was one of the four complainants, the others being John Ridout, Arthur Squib and Robert White.

In 1693/4, Richard Newman, no doubt of the family, if not the same Richard Newman, complained that his estate and land in Stalbridge were over-rated and his Poor Rates were reduced from 30s to 24s 6d.

THE CASE OF SAMUEL RICH, RECTOR OF STALBRIDGE.

When the Earl of Cork bought the Stalbridge Estate, he is said also to have bought the advowson of the living of Stalbridge.

It is presumed that his son, Robert Boyle, inherited this privilege along with the Estate and Manor.

Being very much concerned with the spread of religious knowledge, he must have heard with alarm about the state of confusion in the parish under his own direction, revealed in the following complaint from the parishioners about the behaviour of the Rev Samuel Rich, Rector of St. Mary's, Stalbridge, from 1675.

The complaint took the form of an undated letter to King Charles II. The year, 1687, was entered in the Parish Register, now lost, against Samuel Rich's name; but it is difficult to draw any satisfactory conclusions about this date. According to Squibb, Samuel Rich, installed 1675, had to leave Stalbridge in 1677, and Robert Boyle did not gain the advowson of Stalbridge until 1690, the year before he died, although the document quoted was found amongst Boyle's papers in the British Library.

To the King's most excellent Majesty and to the right Honourable and right worll the Lords and Commons assembled in the High Court of Parliament.

The most humble complaynt and peticon of the Inhabitants and Parishioners of Stalbridge in the County of Dorset.

In most humble manor complayning sheweth that Samuel Rich, clerke, Rector of the Rectory and parish Church of Stalbridge aforesaid is a person of very ill life and conversacon, and hath committed soe many notorious crimes and offences, especially the crimes and offences following (viz &)

for publiquely declareing his Matie that now is to be the Sonn of a whore, and for declareing other grosse scandalous and reproachfull words against him which we are ashamed to sett forth,

for declareing that the knowne lawes and Statutes of this Realme of England are Sanguinary and Caniball or sorely (?) effeet,

for reteyning from several poore laboring people theire accustomed wages.

for oppressing his parishioners and comenceing severall vexacious and needlesse suites against them,

ffor prophaning the Lords dayes comonly called Sunday in rideing greate journyes and afterwards goeing to Church in a very indecent manner and soe nastily that it hath bin very offensive to the parishioners.

ffor often absenting himselfe from his Cure & parish Church, and some time for the space of ffower score dayes together,

ffor pressing or causeing severall of the parishioners horse beasts to be pressed and taken upp for his owne concernes,

ffor threatening the ruine and destruccon of many of his parishioners,

ffor seduceing Elizabeth the wife of Thomas Snooke of Stalbridge aforesaid, Button maker, and comitting the greate Sin of Adultery with her And for marrying himselfe unto her, by reading the forme of the solempnizacon of matrimony unto her And then persuading her that it was not any sin as she the said Elizabeth Snooke by her voluntary confession on her oath before the worll Thomas Chaffe Esq one of his Maties Justices of the peace of this County of Dorset aforesaid hath confessed and acknowledged And for adhereing to the Popish Religon, by haveing bin present at Mass as it is comonly reported

And for severall other notorious crimes and offences, which are soe offensive and preuidiciall to your puore peticoners and divers other parishioners of the said parish, that in the tendernesse of our and theire consciences, wee nor they cannot associate our nor theire selves with him nor frequent our and theire parish Church (when he the said Samuel Rich is present,) as we ought to do nor heare him for feare of being seduced by him And thereby preuidice our and theire precious soules then which nothing is more deare unto us.

And therefore we your humble Peticoners doe most humbly beseech your Matie And you the right Honable Lords, and Comons now assembled in Parliament to take the premisses into your serious consideracon.

And to take such cause that the said samuel Rich may be by your authorityes removed from the said Parsonage & cure of Soules and an honester man put in his place.

And wee and the rest of the protestant parishioners of the said parish (as in Duty bound) shall for ever pray for your Maties and the Lords Comons now assembled in Parliament Length of Dayes prosperity in this life and eternall felicity in that which is to come.

William Weston	Samll Boles Constable
John Coombe	William Looer ? Churchwarden
James Cave	Henery Gerrard Churchwarden
Robert Tyte	Thomas Snooke
Will Tyte Se	Lewis Morgan) Overseirs
Thomas Snooke	Robert Chaffey)
Richard Cliner	Robert Snooke Offiser
William Coombe	Willi Gartrell
Thomas Coombe	Nicholas Watts

Such was the nature of the man that he petitioned against the dismissal under the Act of Indemnity granted by William and Mary. Except for a Clause in the Act by which he lost his appeal because of his adultery, he might have been restored to his living and prosecuted the Divine to whom it had been given.

Not surprisingly, his name appears more than once in local legal suits, suggesting that he was of the nature of a vexatious litigant, arguing his way around a situation, where others would have admitted guilt.

The substance of his Will, written in 1702, long after he left Stalbridge and lived in Woodbridge, Holwell, exposes the eccentricity and unusual philosophy of a man of the cloth.

For information from Dr Williams's Library and the location of the Will, I am deeply grateful to John Findon, of Sale, Cheshire.

After humbly commending his Soul to the mercies of God, he wrote;

I give devise and bequeath unto my said son Samuel Rich all my whole estate both real and personal . . . Upon this condition nevertheless that he my said son Samuel doth marry within one year next after my Decease a person having a Fortune of three thousand pounds and with such her Fortune that he my said Son Samuel doth clear my said Estate and pay all other my just Debts Legacies and Funeral Expenses.

Item I give and bequeath unto my Son Richard Rich my Estates called Rodmore and Staggs provided likewise that he my said Son Richard do within the space of twelve months get a Fortune and thereby clear both the said Estates which if he my said Son Richard Rich shall do then I further give and bequeath unto him my said Son Richard the Estate I have at present in Trims Checks Buffits and Frosts . . .

Item I give unto my said Son Richard the Goods in the Kitchin of his now Dwellinghouse and the Furniture of two of the second best Chambers in the same House.

Item I give unto my loving Wife Mary twenty pounds to buy her Mourning and also the Use of Furniture for two Rooms for her during her Life to be had and taken by her my said Wife out of the House in my said Son Richard's Possession or out of my House at Woodbridge as she my said Wife shall think fit Provided that she gives Security to leave the same Goods to my Executor hereinafter named at the time of her Decease . . .

After several bequests to daughters, grandchildren and servants, Samuel Rich left forty shillings to the poor in the parishes of Sarney, Stalbridge and Holwell.

Two of the beneficiaries of the Will of Samuel Rich, senior, due to receive forty pounds apiece on reaching 'one and twenty years or sooner if my said Executor shall think fitting', were his grandsons, James and Samuel Pranker, sons of James Pranker by his late daughter, Susanna, deceased.

These boys were grandsons also of James Pranker, senior, of Stalbridge, who, together with his sons, Samuel and Joseph, and his daughter Elizabeth, 'all died of a malignant fever in a few days of one another and were interred in one grave' on 13 February, 1694/5.

The tragedy struck the young grandsons yet deeper, when their mother, Susanna, daughter of Samuel Rich, died shortly afterwards and was buried in Stalbridge on 20 March, 1694/5.

How or when the bequests were paid after the death of Samuel Rich is not certain. Both Samuel Rich, senior, and his son, Samuel, were involved in a legal dispute in October, 1704, Gillett v Rich, Stegg & White, wherein the disputed property was conveyed to Samuel Rich of Woodbridge, one of the Defendants. However much the satisfaction gained, Samuel Rich, senior, did not live long after this case. He was buried in Holwell on 7th February, 1704/5 and his Will was proved in August, 1705.

It would be interesting to know whether Samuel, the younger, married his heiress, but after buying the manors of Lydlinch and Hyde and the advowson of Lydlinch from Lord Stourton in 1706, by 1711 he had sold them and various other cottages, farms and tenenments, conveying the 'residue of the same premises to trustees on trust to sell discharging incumbrances'.

His estates in Holwell were under the Receivership in 1727; Lunn v Rich; another legal case in 1728 disclosed that he was then acting as Steward to Lord Stourton.

DENT v YOUNG

A legal dispute in Stalbridge in 1694 involved Thomas Dent, the Rector appointed after the dismissal of Samuel Rich, Clerk. Evidently Roger Young, a yeoman, 'had five years since rented the rectory from Thomas Dent and now sues Andrew Loder of Sturton Caundle, yeoman, for tithes due from 20 acres of arable and 50 acres of pasture in Stalbridge, possessed and occupied by Loder'.

The land was sub-let, but it was not stated whether the Rectory house was included and Thomas Dent an absentee Parson. He was soon replaced in 1694 by Richard Wright, who enjoyed the advantage of living in the large new Rectory built near the Cross in 1699.

HALLETT v STALBRIDGE CHURCHWARDENS & OVERSEERS

The names of seventeenth century Churchwardens and Overseers of the Poor in Stalbridge come to the fore in 1691, when William Hallett of Henstridge made a plea against the officials of Stalbridge who had lent money to three yeomen of Henstridge. By indenture of 1661, the freehold lands of Knowls and Longbrooke at Yewston (Yenston) had been mortgaged to these creditors and William Hallett, descendant, was making a claim for the land.

The Churchwardens were John King and John Carter, the Overseers William Stone, William Duffett, George Hancock and Lawrence Hobbs; also lending money was Elnathan Atkins, Constable of Stalbridge (for Brownshall Hundred).

One might ponder on the inducements that persuaded these men trusted with public responsibility to offer money outside Stalbridge and whether they ever profited by the investment.

KING'S MILL BRIDGE

A hint that the Michaelmas Courts of the Abbot of Sherborne may not have been held in Stalbridge because of the state of the travel was given in 1515 to 1516, although some money was allocated to the improvement of the Sherborne Causeway between Sherborne and Shaftesbury during Elizabeth's reign. It is hardly likely that there was much improvement to the bridge during the seventeenth century and it is only when the more important bridges were in decay that any indication is given of the possible hazards to travel.

During the same year that Sturminster Bridge was said to be in decay in 1673, there was a suggestion that the wooden bridge at King's Mill be replaced by a stone bridge at a cost of £250, and the old timber be sold for the use of the County. A Highway Rate was levied for Stalbridge and a threat of distraining or sale of goods for non-payment of rates.

Unfortunately, the gap in the Quarter Sessions records from 1673 to 1686 does not allow one to assume that the stone bridge was built soon after the order, but by 1688, King's Mill bridge needed gravelling and the causeway to the west (in the parish of Stalbridge) was in decay. The work was ordered to be done at 'the Cheapest Rate'.

By 1699, the bridge was again in decay.

The improvement of King's Mill bridge for the sake of trade in Stalbridge market was not given as a reason until over one hundred years later, but one can judge that the bad state of the bridges in the area would prevent local travel and therefore affect the trade at the local markets and fairs.

The date of King's Mill bridge, an important link for Stalbridge with Marnhull and Sturminster Newton is 1823.

CHANGES AT THE END OF THE SEVENTEENTH CENTURY

The end of the century saw changes in Stalbridge which would ultimately affect the lives of its inhabitants.

The advowson of the living was sold in 1697 by Viscount Shannon, which put the gift of the living of Stalbridge into the hands of Corpus Christi College, Cambridge, instead of the Lord of the Manor, and brought a more energetic Rector in the form of Rev. Richard Wright.

Robert Boyle as Lord of the Manor for nearly fifty years until 1691, well occupied elsewhere with scientific investigations, had shown little interest affecting property or acquiring land. Peter Walter, the new Lord of the Manor at the end of the century was less of a gentleman and more of a man of property with eyes on advancement.

SIXTEEN

The New Lords of the Manor

A round the turn of the seventeenth century, Stalbridge Manor and estate passed out of the hands of Robert Boyle's brothers and heirs. In May 1699, the name of Peter Walter, gent, of St. Margaret's, Westminster, appeared on the Mortgage document of the Manor with that of the Rt. Hon. Richard Boyle, Lord Viscount Shannon.

Francis, Viscount Shannon, was responsible for paying the Stalbridge Church Rate in 1695, so he may have continued to use the house 'kept up' by his brother for his sake, but in 1697, he sold the advowson of the manor to Archbishop Tenison who gave it to Corpus Christi College, Cambridge, in whose gift it has remained ever since.

Lord Shannon died before January 1699. Mrs Elizabeth Boyle, possibly his widow, in debt for £566.15s. had in 1695, assigned the payment by annuity following his death to Richard Turner. In 1699, Richard Turner assigned the debt and payment to Peter Walter. Although Francis, Lord Shannon, was Court Baron of Stalbridge, Peter Walter was holding Court in 1697 as Steward, most of the cases that year dealing with heriots and reversions.

Francis, Lord Shannon, was succeeded by his grandson, Richard, Viscount Shannon, his own son, Richard, having predeceased him. Richard, Viscount Shannon, was recorded as Court Baron until 1699 when he was succeeded by Francis Child, (a London Banker), with Peter Walter acting as Steward.

The debt of Mrs Elizabeth Boyle no doubt gave Peter Walter considerable pressure on the gaining of the Stalbridge Manor.

Few facts are known about Peter Walter's early life, but an enquiry by the Steward of the Dorset and Somerset Estate in the early nineteenth century revealed that he had been born in Wyke Champflower, near Bruton, in Somerset. Present-day enquiries have yielded little, but it is likely that he was the son of Peter Walter of Wyke Champflower, who died in 1696, leaving his son, Peter, and his wife, the sum of two shillings and sixpence.

In 1696/7, Peter Walter had for more than ten years been Steward to Richard Newman of the Manor of Fifehead Magdalen, a few miles from Stalbridge, and was obviously well acquainted with manorial estate work. His experience also included estate management for the Earls of Uxbridge and the Duke of Newcastle. Walter was described by Hutchins in his *History of Dorset* as a man who would not lend money or buy land without seeing every acre. He was reputed to have told James West,

'I live on bread and butter, and milk porridge; and it must be land that maintains the cows for this: whereas none of the stock companies have a single cow.'

Peter Walter acquired an immense fortune in his lifetime, and with it, certain notoriety. He is presumed to have been the original of Peter Pounce in Henry Fielding's first published novel, *The History of the Adventures of Joseph Andrews, and of his Friend Mr Abraham Adams.*

Fielding grew up in East Stour, quite close to Fifehead Magdalen, where Peter Walter had been Steward, and began as a playwright in London, ending his career as a dramatist by his outspoken political criticism, and then turning to law and journalism. The character of the acquisitive and rascally steward, Peter Pounce, appeared in print in 1742. Pope also referred to Peter Walter but it was as a 'dextorous attorncy.'

In his story, *Squire Petrick's Lady*, Thomas Hardy depicted the owner of Stapleford (Stalbridge) Park as that

'trump of mortgages . . . whose skill in gaining possession of fair estates by granting sums of money on title deeds has seldom been equalled in our part of England.'

He described him as having to walk over every acre with his own two feet, prodding 'the soil at every point with his own spud' before he would buy land, a clear reference to Peter Walter of Stalbridge.

Of Peter Walter, Lord of the Manor of Stalbridge, and his long connection with Stalbridge, little is revealed except through information from surviving deeds and wills.

A survey of Stalbridge in 1705 was ordered by the Lord of the Manor and taken by William Drew of the dwellings and closes on the 1724 acres of his Stalbridge Estate. A further Survey of the manor of Stalbridge was completed for Peter Walter in 1719, and there is a special entry for the 'Manor House, Garden, Orchard, Courtyard and Park, 50 acres.' The number of tenants in Stalbridge had increased to 160, renting 1834 acres.

Several particulars are included of small estates under 100 acres purchased by Peter Walter from their owners, which, together with details of leases and sales, suggest a continuous investment in land and property in North Dorset and Somerset.

Unfortunately, there is no description of the 'goodlie faire house' built by Castlehaven and enlarged by Cork, in the papers left by the Walter family. Hutchins believed that the House was 'much improved' by Peter Walter. The size and situation of the Park surrounding the large Manor House can be verified from a section of a map drawn in 1738 by Edward Curray, a school master of Stalbridge, twenty years before the enclosure of the New Park shown in the Map of 1760.

How often Walter came to Stalbridge is uncertain; his address was given as St. Margaret's, Westminster, when Sir Francis Child took a lease of the Manor of Stalbridge in 1712. His interests in Dorset did not only extend to Stalbridge. Following the Act of 1711, it was possible for Peter Walter on acquiring land to become an M.P. even though he was not of the landed gentry. In 1715, he became M.P. for Bridport, in place of Sir Dewey Bulkeley, and seven years later, he was M.P. for Bridport with Sir Dewey Bulkeley, kt.

It is hardly surprising, in the midst of all the intense anchoring of property and land, to find in the Court Book of Sturminster Newton Castle for 1735 and 1736, complaints about Peter Walter's encroachment upon the land of Geo Pitt Esq near Southly and Manston. As late as 1754 and 1757, Edward Walter was still accused of withholding and detaining pieces of land belonging to Geo Pitt Esq, and there is no entry to show whether the matter was ever resolved.

At the end of his long life in 1745, Peter Walter, aged 83, requested that his body should be buried in St. Mary's Church, Stalbridge, in the vault in the aisle belonging to his Manor House.

He stated in his Will that from the mortgage on Michael Harvey's several manors of Clifton, Bradford and Wyke there was due to him thirty three thousands pounds over and above the money due from the mortgaging of Harvey's manor of Combe, which shows the extent of some of the money transactions in which he had been engaged.

Michael Harvey had the misfortune to die before a wealthy relative from whom he would have inherited £4,000 per year and been released from a great deal of his debt to Peter Walter.

Bequests by Peter Walter of £5 each were made to three domestic servants and £50 per year to Thomas Swan for holding his Courts and keeping his estate accounts, and he left £5 to be distributed to the poor of Stalbridge and £5 to the poor of Hanley where he had another dwelling house.

His estate was reputed to be worth £300,000, which passed to three grandsons and their male heirs, his son having died in his lifetime. He was succeeded by his oldest grandson, Peter, who died only eight years later leaving no male issue.

The most significant contribution of the younger Peter Walter to the history of Stalbridge was the Survey he ordered in 1749, but in spite of a note on the back page indicating 'Improved values', no explanation was given of any rent increases or upgrading. Gardens were not assessed under a quarter of an acre, but it is surprising to find that the total acreage of land rented had been reduced since the 1719 Survey.

Very little is recorded about Peter Walter, grandson. A Deed of Separation shows that he and his wife, Christian, must have separated in 1752, not long before his death in 1753. In his Will, Peter Walter revealed his grandfather's wishes with regard to the disposition of the Dorset and Somerset Estates, of which Stalbridge with its Manor House was the focal centre.

Ignoring the female descendants, the inheritance was to pass from the Walter grandsons, failing male issue, to the sons of Sir Nicholas Bayly, who had taken the name of Paget from their mother's line of descent and owned Plas Newydd in Anglesey.

The second Peter Walter's lack of investment and selling of property was noted fifty years later by Robert James, Agent to the Stalbridge Estate, who suggested or repeated hearsay that it was due to the disposition of his grandfather's Estates, failing male Walter issue. The second Peter Walter had no son. It must be stated that there are records of a few transactions in his period of Lordship of the Manor, and from the Will of his sister, Mary Walter, it is obvious that he lived in the Manor House and that she lived with him. Her bequests included £10 each to his servants who had been in the House for at least three years.

Edward, the youngest grandson, inherited the estates from his brother, Peter, Sheldon, the second grandson, having already pre-deceased him. Several deeds in the Hertfordshire Record Office reveal that Edward continued to buy land and extend the family estates in Dorset and Somerset.

That he displayed more than a passing interest in his Dorset inheritance is indicated by his application to the Dorset Quarter Sessions in 1756, to enclose land around his Mansion, some leased to tenants, as well as the late Mr Weston's Farm, an area enclosing an old Manor House of the tything of Weston, and certain highways.

The new enclosure was planned to spread north to Landshire Lane, west to Green Lane and south-west to Barrow Hill and New Lane, (the walk between the Church and Barrow Hill), in extent almost ten times the area of the old Stalbridge Park, enclosed in 1618 by Mervyn Lord Audley, Earl of Castlehaven, after a long legal battle with the inhabitants. It was proposed to cut off old established routes to Sherborne and Henstridge which ran across the new Park.

The application was received in Sherborne at the April meeting of the Dorset Quarter Sessions, which Edward Walter attended as a Justice of the Peace. Following a fashionable movement of the time by great landowners of 'emparking', but somewhat ahead of Lord Milton, (1763), and Sir Gerard Napier, (1764) at Moor Critchell, permission was granted. It was found that enclosure would not 'damage the King or travellers' because two other roads or highways 'branch out or divide near the said roads'. It meant, in effect, that travellers would no longer be able to use the old Sherborne Road to Landshire Lane, nor to take short cuts from Stalbridge to the Henstridge Road, but would have to travel farther around the outer perimeters of the newly enclosed Park.

According to the map of the Park drawn to scale in 1760, Trustees dealt with the leases of land newly enclosed by the Wall, which had been built to surround the new Park. This wall, traditionally believed by some to have been built by French prisoners of the War, though often repaired, still stands, its five mile length of dry-laid coursed rubble protecting the Park and remaining a dominant feature alongside the highways which almost encircle it.

There is no record of official protests after the enclosure of Stalbridge Park in 1760, similar to the one brought against Lord Audley in 1618.

Following the death of Edward Walter in 1780, there being no male heirs, the Stalbridge estate and other properties, left in reversion by the will of Peter Walter, 1752, descended to Henry Paget, son of Sir Nicholas Bayly, of Plas Newydd, Anglesey, who, on his legal documents, added the name of Peter Walter. So far, the reason why Peter Walter made this direction, 'to take and use the name of Peter Walter', remains unresolved.

Edward Walter's Will reveals little about the Stalbridge Estate, but rather more about his property at Berry Hill, Surrey, where he preferred to be buried, instead of in the Walter Vault in Stalbridge Church.

The mystery of the gift of the Stalbridge Estate to the Pagets of Plas Newydd, Anglesey remains. In his biographical account of the family of Henry-William, the first Marquis of Anglesey, who inherited the estates from his father, Henry Paget, the present Marquis offers three connections between the Walter family and the Pagets and Baylys, but, he adds, in his book entitled, *One Leg*, 'they do no more than accentuate the mystery which surrounds the relationship:

1. Peter Walter (grandfather) was at one time steward to 1st Earl of Uxbridge (of the first creation) who died in 1743.

2. The father of the Peter Walter who made the Will was Paget Walter.

3. Up to her death in 1828, an annuity of £300 was paid by the head of the Paget family to Mrs Bullock, the only child of the Peter Walter who made the Will.'

It is intriguing also to find an early possible Paget connection in Dorset where, in St. Gregory's Church, Marnhull, in a small vault was buried one body, 'supposed to be the body of the honourable Henry Paget, brother to Lord Paget, Baron of Beaudesert who was buried Mar 13, 1709.'

There is another interesting factor which has only recently come to light. In the Will of Thomas Paget, third son of William, Lord Paget, and grandson of the Earl of Uxbridge, dated Stalbridge 11 October, 1716, which was proved on 15 January, 1728/9, this 'affectionately faithfull gratefull friend' of Peter Walter, (grandfather), appointed him to be his 'sole heir and executor', bequeathing him whatever belonged to him (Thomas Paget), 'or may be due . . . from any source whatsoever.'

Further investigation outside Dorset may yet uncover reasons why the Walter estates were later bequeathed to the Pagets. The possession of the Dorset and Somerset Estates of the Walter family, together with the Beaudesert and Staffordshire properties, and the Welsh Estates, meant that Henry Bayly Paget Peter Walter, created Earl of Uxbridge in 1784, had control over 100,000 acres of land.

Twelve years before the Walter bequest was inherited, Henry Bayly Paget had already in anticipation applied for a loan using the Dorset and Somerset Estates as securities but the result is not known.

After the death of Edward Walter in 1780, his son-in-law, Lord Grimston, married to his daughter, Harriet, was engaged in correspondence with Lord Paget regarding the house at Stalbridge. He and his wife must have stayed there for in October, 1780, he was asked by Lord Paget, who was due to travel into Dorsetshire, where the keys of the writings might be found as Mr Grimston had told him that the 'all the papers' were at the House at Stalbridge.

By 1782, Lord Paget's Agent had collected rentals and complained that some timber had been cut in '7 and 20 years', only to be reminded by Lord Grimston that the rentals from Leaseholds granted by the 'late Mr Walter' in his lifetime, were due to Lady Grimston.

The difficulties concerning the smaller details such as the one above must have been numerous and time-consuming, but by April, 1783, Lord Grimston was about to auction the remainder of the furniture belonging to him and his wife at Stalbridge and was offering a picture of the 'young Peter Walter' for which Lord Paget had given an 'inclination' that he wished to possess it.

Lord Grimston wrote concernedly that in a 'Business of Magnitude', some parts of it were moving so slowly that the whole would be a long time before it was finished, adding

'my great anxiety to have it compleated will exculpate me, however, from the Idea that I have a wish to put any impediment in the Way of it, and there is nothing I wish more than to convince Your Lordship that I do not.'

It appears that there was some awkwardness in the matter of handing over, but it is unlikely that the house was afterwards used as permanent home by Lord Paget, created Earl of Uxbridge in 1784, whose other seats were Plas Newydd in Anglesey, Beaudesert, Staffordshire, and a house in St. James's Square, London.

After 1783, there is no surviving correspondence to show how the matters progressed between Lord Paget and Lord Grimston, acting on behalf of his wife, Harriet Walter, but the Estates were finally recovered legally in 1791.

A Schedule of plans drawn up for the Earl of Uxbridge in 1789, showed that the estates extended into at least 18 Dorset villages and others in Somerset and Wiltshire, and new properties were bought during the next few years; some letters from Robert James, the Agent, to the Earl of Uxbridge reveal the business in property dealings. Baskets of game from his Dorset estate were evidently appreciated by the Earl when he was in Windsor and London.

The list of villages in Dorset and Somerset owned by Lord Paget, created 1st Earl of Uxbridge of the 2nd creation in 1784, is impressive.

The Manors of Stalbridge, Anteox, Weston, Handley, Gussage St. Andrew, Clifton Maybank, Bradford Abbas and Manston; messuages etc in these manors and Farnham, Gussage St. Michael Iwerne, Stour Provost, Stourpaine, Marnhull, Kington Magna, West Stour, Over and Nether Compton, Thornford, Hammoon and Sturminster Newton, and advowsons of Fifehead Neville and Manston (Dorset); hundreds of Charlton Horethorn and Norton Ferris, manors of Milborne Port, Milborne Wick, Kingsbury Regis, Henstridge, Yenston, Temple Coombe and Abbas Coombe, messuages in these and Cheriton and Horsington, (Somerset).

More descriptively, it was interpreted as:
400 messuages; 10 mills; 20 dovehouses; 400 gardens; 8,000 acres of land; 2,000 acres of meadow; 4,000 acres of pasture; 1,000 acres wood; 5,000 acres furze & heath; 1,000 acres moor; 500 acres land covered with water.

The possession by the new Lord of the Manor of several estates and established homes in Plas Newydd, Anglesey, Beaudesert, Staffordshire and London, proved to be unfortunate for Stalbridge House, which, unwanted as a family retreat, had disappeared by 1825.

SEVENTEEN

The Parish Registers

It is recorded that the first legible entry in the Parish Register was that of a Thornhill, dated 1540. Unfortunately, the first Register appears to have been lost after the publication of the first edition of Hutchins.

In his short history of Stalbridge, 1889, Rev. W.S. Swayne wrote that the first register had been lost for more than thirty years.

Hutchins recorded that under the year 1653 there was the entry *Equibus temporibus liberet nos Dominus* (From which times may the Lord deliver us). The entry was no doubt made by Rector, John Douch, who in the same year recorded that John King had been chosen by the parishioners of Stalbridge to take the register.

John Douch was ejected from the living and his place was taken by one Nathaniel Fairclough, 'who treated him very ill and allowed him not the fifths, which were supposed to be devoted to the support of the ejected clergy.' Nathaniel Fairclough was married and buried in Long Burton. His memorial records him as 'Rector Ecclesiae Stalbrigiensis died 11 October, 1656'.

The earliest surviving register dates from 1690 and Swayne noted that the names entered in the first two years were almost all represented still in Stalbridge in 1889: viz. Galpin, Tyte, Lamon, Duffett, Snooke, Jeans, Clark, Harris, Sinyovr, Oliver, Drew, West, Parsons, Brown, Rogers, Vining, Shepard, Poole. Indeed, many of these surnames survive today.

In order to protect the woollen trade, burials had to be in woollen with Affidavits normally provided, the form of which is given in the front of the Register.

A few entries from the Register are given here, although there are certain years when details would have enlightened us about the conditions under which people lived and died. Other tragedies need no explanation.

1699, Jan 26. Glory be to God. Dinah Masters, my servt. aged 22 years, baptized in Stalbridge Church.

BURIALS
1703 Apr 1 A Vagrant Woman Drown'd in the River.

1707 Jan 27 Anne, wife of Ezekiel Pool) These 3 died of the small Pox
1707 Feb 1 Anne, wife of John Pool   ) & tho' buried in Woollen had
John, son of John Pool   ) no Affidavits.
1713 Feb 13 Wm Weston Senr Esq. Buried in Linen
1715 Dec 11 Morgan Merrick A Welch Man.
1731 May 10 Betty, daughter of Dr Richard Wright.
1731 May 15 Mary, wife of Dr.Richard Wright.
1734 May 10 Sir James Thornhill Knight
1743 Jan 9 Trephenah & Trephosa Dowding (Bap Dec 28)
1745 Jan 29 Peter Walter Esq.
1778 Dec 6 Betty Clarke out of her mind
1778 Dec 18 Betty & Sarah Brown Drown'd
1779 Sep 11 John Duffett died in a Well
1779 Sep Wm Ann & Joseph, 3 children of Wm & Betty Haine-in one
grave
1784 Oct 8 John Curtis killed by a Waggon

It is a sad reflection that where once there was a Thornhill Chapel on the south side of the choir in which many Thornhills were buried, not a sign remains of the tomb of Sir James Thornhill, one of Stalbridge's famous men.

Nor is there a trace of the vault that Peter Walter created for his dynasty, although there is evidence that it was re-opened for a burial in the early nineteenth century.

A reminder of the change of calendar to New Style is given in a rather late notice:

1756 Mem. ye 4 children for Jan. Feb. Mar. 1757 are to begin ye yr 1757, to bring ye Register to New Style wch shd have been done before.

THE BLEAK YEARS

Several years throughout the eighteenth century had record burial figures which must have alarmed the population of Stalbridge and been the result of much sickness and suffering. Yet on only two occasions are reasons given, in the 1690s when there was a malignant fever, and in 1707, when there was an outbreak of small-pox which was probably contained as the yearly death rate was only half of that in 1712. In that year, the number of burials rose dramatically to 53, the average rate during the first decade of the century being less than half this number.

No reasons can be found for the 1712 increase, Marnhull, the nearest village recording only the normal number of deaths. It is known from Hutchins, however, that Milton Abbas suffered a great loss of persons during that year from small-pox.

The years 1729 and 1742 again saw the number of burials in Stalbridge rise to over 50, the number in December, January and February, 1729/30 reaching 21. Marnhull also suffered an increase, the number in the same months reaching 16. Speculation as to causes is endless as during this period there were national outbreaks of agues and influenza as well as the usual round of infectious diseases.

Although the numbers of burials in the winter months on 1742/3 reached 24, out of a total of 56 for the year, from June to the following March there was an high incidence of deaths in families, with two people of the same surname dying within days of each other. This year was one in which small pox was rife throughout England.

It is following the years 1765, 1766 and 1767, again years with small pox attacking on a national scale, when Stalbridge with higher than average numbers, over 40, saw some initiative in the parish.

In 1767 the Stalbridge Overseers consented to pay

'. . . Mr Charles Green Sur 6 gns a year to take care and look after the Poor of the Parish in case of sickness for one year ensuing. (Surgery & Broken Bones if Capable of doing.)'

By 1771, however, it was

'Agreed by the Vestry with Mr Chas Green & Mr Robt Grimshaw to inoculate all the poor people at 3s a piece & to warn that they shall have the Small Pox By their Inoculation so that they shall not have it again to the Detriment of the Town
    as Witness Our Hands
    John Hobbs Thos Burge John Lewis Wm Brown Thos Bartlett'

The date is significant here as it was before 1774, when Benjamin Jesty in Worth Matravers inoculated his own wife and children with the cow pox to prevent them getting small pox, and long before Jenner's investigations in the 1780s and 1790s.

How well the inoculations worked is not recorded, nor what was used. However, the idea of inoculations had been introduced as early as 1717 by the traveller, Lady Mary Wortley Montague, who had seen successful inoculations against smallpox in Turkey. The principle was well established throughout the country after being accepted by Royalty during succeeding years and in 1771, it became established in Stalbridge.

In spite of the high death rate amongst children (in 1705 out of 26 burials, 12 were of children, including 5 babies under 3 months), Stalbridge had its share of long-livers, who, dying towards the end of the century, had all survived the scourges and diseases mentioned above.

The list is impressive, but selective, and includes only those over 80 years of age:

    1785 Apr 24 Susannah Paine aged 90
    Oct 2 Thos Hunt aged 85
    Nov 1 Matthew Burge aged 92
    1786 Apr 11 Edward Dober aged 84
    1787 Feb 9 Elizabeth Allen aged 87

1793 Feb 3 Sarah Oliver aged 84
1795 Jan 24 Mary Watts aged 91
1795 Feb 15 Ann Jeans aged 91

From the memoranda at the beginning of the Overseers Account Book OV/4, it is clear that a doctor was appointed for looking after the Poor of Stalbridge. In 1799, John Coombs agreed to duties outlined below;

'I hereby engage to take proper care of the Poor of the Parish of Stalbridge @ 20 Guineas per year, Except Small Pox, Compound Fractures, Extra case of Midwifery, (more than 24 hours), Journeys out of the Parish, Medicines not to be Paid for, Venereal Complaints, Accidents happening to Strangers Passing through the Parish.'

A memorandum of April 27, 1800 added:–

'Mr Coombs is not required to attend any common cases of Midwifery, and will allow out of the above salary, 15/- for the said cases, provided there happens six in a year at 2/6 each.'

EIGHTEEN

Churchwardens' Accounts

The first book of Churchwardens' Accounts, 1694-1761, now sadly in rather a worn state, reveals payments to the poor, the Church being responsible for paying the poor by an Act of 1601, and other parish commitments.

The first page of payments gives examples of monies distributed and of the number of people passing through Stalbridge expecting charity.

(The daily dates were not always entered.)

1695 Disbursed by Samll Bowles and William Langdon, Chw

May 10 given to a poore man and his family being cast away at sea, having a pass	1s 0d
May 11 given a Quartermaster of horse and 10 men having a pas	1s 0d
paid Tho.Turk one hedgog	2d
John Ellinor 4 hedgog	8d
Browns Boy 1 hedgog	2d
Edw. Jollose 2 hedgog	4d
a poore man and his wife having a pas	6d
a pore woman and a child having a pass	6d
Boy Clark for a hedgog	2d
for a man and his wife for quarters, by pas	1s 2d
Tho Turk 2 hedgogs	4d
a poore woman having a pass	4d
Joseph Semes for painting the pulpit	12s 6d
4 poore men by pas	6d
Barritt for a fox	1s 0d
Tho Tvrk	12d

It was permissible to pay something to wounded soldiers, sailors, or the poor having a pass, that is a permit to travel, even though each parish at that time was responsible through the Act of Settlement for its own poor.

The Account Book begins in 1694 during the period of William III's war with France when 90,000 men were engaged. The decisive victories were at sea where England showed the mastery of her naval strategies which helped to end the war in 1697. The cost in men is reflected in the following entries: -

1695 Paid 11 wounded souldrej (soldiers) having a paz
May 22, 1696, Pd to 14 maym'd seamen yt came out of ffrance –
passe 00.00.06d
1696 Pd a maym'd seaman yᵗ was a prisoner in ffrance 00.00.00½d.'

The year, 1696, saw the introduction of the new coinage and the way of entering the money changed to double figures which included the noughts – 00.00.06d.

The payment to passers-by ceased in 1699, only to be resumed again in 1721, when as many as 116 seamen were relieved as they passed through Stalbridge. In 1719 England had been engaged in brief naval warfare with Spain and Captain Byng defeated the Spanish fleet off Cape Passaro, Sicily, with peace concluded in 1720, which probably accounts for the influx of seamen.

The Wars in 1745, one a lingering war with France in which the English were defeated at Fontenoy, and then the invasion of England by the men supporting the Stuart cause under Charles Edward, and the defeat of the Highlanders at Culloden, could have left their toll on the numbers seeking relief in Stalbridge in 1747 . . .

1747 10 wounded sailors	5s 0d
12 wounded men	12s 0d
18 sick & wounded men	5s 0d
6 wounded men	2s 6d

The Churchwardens were also responsible for making payments for creatures regarded by the parish as vermin. From some entries, it would seem that they had to keep a perpetual bonfire if they were not to have heaps of decaying heads or bodies left around.

The wild life in Stalbridge must have been tremendously depleted, when as many as 5½ dozen sparrow heads and 1 hedgehog could be collected by one man or boy, for which John Rownell in 1695 was paid 1s 1d, and, in 1698, Silas Jenkins collected 10d for 1 polecat's head and 3 dozen sparrows' heads.

In 1724 the sum was stated as follows

'What Mr George Snook layed out for varmint 9s 2d'

The year 1726 was particularly productive of dead victims, which included 671 sparrows, 74 hedgehogs, 3 martens, 2 polecats and 1 otter.

Probably the folklore surrounding the creatures such as hedgehogs accounted more for the vengeance wreaked, rather than the actual damage by the creatures themselves. Other 'varments' collected included foxes, martens and otters; for all creatures there was a set rate which remained the same throughout the period of the first Churchwarden's Account Book, payment rates for sparrows being 2d per dozen, hedgehogs 2d each, stoats 2d each, polecats 4d each, martens and foxes 1s each.

In 1755 the toll of victims was
10 polecats & 1 stote   3s 6d

43 doz sparrows heads   7s 2d

51½ doz   "   "   8s 7d

James Cole 6 doz " "   1s 0d

There were times, however, when privileges were stopped by order. In 1703, payments for vermin ceased, but resumed again in 1721, and in 1889 when the Rev. W.S. Swayne published his book on Stalbridge, he recorded that the custom had continued until within 'living memory'.

From 1703, nothing was to be allowed for Ringing, which had included the 30th January, the anniversary of the execution of Charles I, and 29th May, Oak Apple Day, and a reminder of the Restoration of Charles II.

Upon the Victory of the Duke of 'Marlobery' – that is Marlborough – at Blenheim in 1704, however, the Ringers were once again in action and on 9th August were paid 3s. In August 1714, the ringers proclaimed the new Hanoverian King, George I, and two months later, his Coronation Day. In 1715, the bells were rung upon the defeat of rebels in Scotland supporting the Roman Catholic 'Old Pretender'.

By 1720 the Accounts expressly state payments for 'Beer on the King's Birthday 2s 6d', which increased to 7s 6d on Proclamation Day and dropped again to 6s 0d on Coronation Day.

Thus was Stalbridge kept abreast of national events, and reminded of its loyalty to the establishment, but it is doubtful whether the new popular form of communication – there were seven newspapers in existence when Queen Anne died, only one when she began her reign in 1702, – had been seen by anyone in Stalbridge except the Lord of the Manor, who had lived in London.

Nor would Stalbridge understand much of the War of the Spanish Succession which continued for much of the reign of the stolid, gouty Queen, who gave birth to many children of whom sadly none survived to succeed. However, the bells rang on 'ye rejoicing day' in 1713 to mark the end of the War and the ringers were paid an extra large sum of £1.

BRIEFS

As well as national events, there was a constant drawing upon the charity of the inhabitants in the briefs given Royal consent for the collection of monies to help in local disasters elsewhere in England.

This encouraged a widening of public sympathy and extended the outlook of people beyond their own locality. It must, however, have meant a great sacrifice on the part of many in the Stalbridge congregations.

In 1694, there was 'Collected for relief of ffrench Protestants' the sum of £1 12s 4d and white farthings of one shilling & sevenpence'.

The 'white' farthings may have been the old silver coinage, changed in 1696 because the silver was gradually being clipped and coins therefore devalued. The number of persons subscribing white farthings could have been as many as 76.

Fires or accidents in churches were collected for, some as far away as Ireland and as far north as Darlington, Co Durham. There was also a collection which raised 10s 0d for a sea-break destroying 500 acres of land in Norfolk.

From details of payments included in the Accounts, it is possible to add certain features to the picture of Stalbridge in the early eighteenth century.

Stalbridge was not without its timepiece; by 1700, the small market town already had its clock with chimes for rousing the inhabitants to work, or other more celebratory activities, and for instilling a sense of time routine.

1696 Recd of Alex Dyer Churchwarden the sum on Three pounds for a new Barrel and other materials about ye Chimes at Stalbridge
John Biddlescombe
1703 Pd for 5½ days works 8s 0d to John Bastable for mending clock, locks etc.

1712 Paid for lock for Clock House and for nailing it on	1s 6d
the rope about ye Chims	8d
1725 Pd William Babstock attending to the Dial	£1.10s 0d
In drink to him and the joiners	3s 0d
1729 new chimes	£3 0s 0d
1733 Oyl & Twine for the Clock & Chimes	3s 0d
1750 Tho Crew Mending the Pendulum	6d

Inside the church, a new gallery was set up in 1721:

1721 For setting up a new gallery for singers at ye West End of ye Church	£16
Mr Wright's gift towards new gallery	16s 0d

There must however, have been another gallery elsewhere in the church because 3 boards were required for 'the old gallery in 1729, and by 1730, there were 'Defects in new gallery seats' repairs to which cost 1s 10d. During the same year, the interior of the church was possibly suffering from leaks in the roof;

Pd for repairing wt was washd out on ye Arches between ye Pillars	12s 6d

Following the addition of a new gallery, in 1734 a new pulpit was erected:

1734 Presentment of the pulpit	1s 0d
Riteing the pulpit and materials for same	11s 0d

In 1723, Mr Wright ordered that 'a woman with child' should be given the sum of 2s 0d. Mr Wright was Rev. Richard Wright, the first Rector to live in the new Rectory built near the Cross in 1699.

He received payment of 5s 0d for keeping the Register and another of 5s 0d 'for keeping his Book'.

The more general payments for articles for church use and work about the church give some idea of comparative prices; books and Holland cloth, for instance, were very expensive compared with men's labour.

Ordinary workmen about the church received 1s for a day's wages; a boy helping them worked 10 days for 3s 4d; one bottle of communion wine cost 2s 6d.

1695 paid Will Drew's wife for washing and mending of the Church Linen	2s 6d
Will Drew's wife for oyle	3s od
1696 Pd Tho Locke for bread for communion	00.01.08d
1696 Pd Mr John Conyer one years' Goal money	01.17.00.
1698 Paid ½ yrs wages for being clerk to Will Sherring	00.06s.08d
1703 Pd ½ yr gail money	£1. 9s.2d
1713 Aug 6 for one skin of vellum for register	2s 6d
For a cloth for Communion Table & Desk	£1 9s 6d
day's wages for work about church	1s od
Nov 12 for beare for workmen in church	
George Pool allowed 2½d per foot for oaken board	
Edward Hillier " 3d " " " " "	
1715 oyle for the bells	
cleansing away the snow to go to church	
1717 Paid Mr Wickham for mending the silver bowl	6s od
Paid 1s od for carrying and bringing the Church Bible to & from Shirburn.	
Paid Richard Gillingham for 3 Bells Ropes	10s od
Paid 16s od for new Comon Prayer Book	
1718 Pd for cleansing yᵉ Church Plate	6d

(Swayne's note in 1889 stated that the Church silver was of more recent date than the 17th century, so presumably the silver bowl, mended in 1717, and the Church Plate above did not survive.)

1723 Pd for confining yᵉ Pidgens out of Church	1s od
1726 Pd Hen Penney for a Pinikell upon the tower	10s od
Pd Chr Snook for collring the Pinikell & lid	15s 6d
1727 Pd 2 yd of Holland for mending the surplis	
Gave workmen a pint of Ale each day	1s 10d
1730 Pd for 15ft of rush mat	3s 2d
Pd John Bidlecome for eaten & dreken	1s od
Acount one journey to Blandford for yᵉ church warden offices & Witnesses	15s 6d
Jacob & Elizabeth Bushes presented at Blandford for Adultery	19s 4d
1733 Pd to Thomas Hobbs ½ yᵉ charge of releasing Edward Beazly from Bridwel	9s 6d
& attending & executing of same	8s 8d
9 Bottles of Wine & 6 Loaves used at Christmas	£1 3s 6d
1734 Expences carrying down to Beaminster the goal mony	2s od
10½yds of Holland at 4s per yd	£2 2s od

Pd for making the surplis   10s 0d
1747 Allowed Clerk salary instead of collecting the Groats
Pd Lott Gattrell   £3 6s 8d

CHURCH RATE

The payment of these sums for very varying purposes was only possible because of the collection of a Church Rate. Rates were levied on certain dwellings and pieces of land. Only a few of these lists are contained in the first Churchwarden's Account Book. The total Rate collected in 1719 from the four tithings of Stalbridge was £23 10s 6d, unaltered from 1695.

In 1695, Stalbridge Town Tithing listed 99 names of rates assessed, Gomages 14 names; Weston 37 names and Thornhill 24 names.

Some of the people may have paid more than one rate depending on the pieces of land they occupied and the dwellings they were responsible for.

Other monies were collected when people were buried and for a time, burial was allowed inside the church for higher fees, 6s 8d for an adult and 3s 4d for a child.

> 1698 Rec'd of Mr Tho Tyw the Eld^r for burying his child in
> church   3s 4d
> 1714 Nicholas Watts wife buried in church   6s 8d

(In 1696, Nicholas Watts had been Churchwarden, and during the lifetime of Robert Boyle, he had been 'Bayliffe of the Manor' of Stalbridge, being remembered in Boyle's Will.)

It was possible also to buy pews, another source of income for the church. The following entry is self-explanatory.

> 1752 June 26 Sold Mr Geo Tite a Pew on left hand of the Wake (Walk) coming into the church for the lives of Benj Vinning, J^n Vinning & Ann Vinning at the purchase of 7s 6d and after the expiration of the three lives to return to ye Parish.

STALBRIDGE CHARITIES

BOYLE'S WILL

By his Will, Robert Boyle bequeathed money to the poor of Stalbridge. Robert Boyle died on 30th December 1691, but a Court in Chancery in 1697 had to make an order for the distribution of the Boyle bequests.

Searches have not been able to reveal how much money came to the Stalbridge poor, the first Churchwardens' Account Book dates from 1694, and there is no entry of money received from the Boyle Bequest after this date.

Boyle had intended that the sum of three hundred pounds be used for the poor of Stalbridge and Fermoy in Ireland.

Ferdinando Touchet, brother of Mervyn, Earl of Castlehaven, was the benefactor of the Charity bearing his name. His bequest of £100 to the poor of Stalbridge was the subject of the case WILLOUGHBY v ANCKETILL in 1639, mentioned in the chapter on the Seventeenth Century.

The Churchwarden's Accounts show that a gift of £20 was entered in 1696 as Ellis's Charity, but no other details are given. Members of the Ellis family were living in Stalbridge at this time, John Ellis had been buried in 1694, but no conclusions may be safely drawn. Hugh Ellis was a weaver in 1659, and in the distribution of Ellis's Charity money on May 30th, 1696, – £1 interest on the sum of £20 – 27 people received 6d or 1s, including one Hugh Ellis, poor, who received 1s.

According to the Churchwarden's Account Book, there was in 1752, an

'acknowledgement of receipt in full of Ferdinando's Money	£100
" " " " " Ellis's Money	£25
which was deposited in Mr Plowman's hand.'	

but no further explanation was added.

Both charities were mentioned in the Parliamentary Returns of 1786, and it was supposed then that in 1756, the parish used the principal of the gifts to purchase the lease of premises, immediately converted into a workhouse, following which, from 1758, the sum of £5.15s was paid from the poor rates and small amounts were distributed to people not receiving parish relief.

The Report to the Charity Commissioners 1818–1837 stated that there was no documentation showing the origin of Ferdinando's and Ellis's Charities, both mentioned in the Parliamentary Returns of 1786.

Payment was kept up until 1830, when it was discontinued following the death of the last surviving life named in the lease.

NINETEEN

Stalbridge Dissenters

In 1662, Richard de Shute, an intruder, was ejected from the Rectory of St. Mary's Church for Nonconformity. This is the first evidence of a Dissenter in Stalbridge, but during the years of toleration that followed the Restoration of King Charles II, and the repealing of the death sentence for heretics, a certain section of the Stalbridge community was dedicated to the Nonconformist movement, for in 1672, John Goffe obtained a licence to hold services in the house of the widow, Ruth Rokcliffe.

In Dr William's Library in London a manuscript, dated 1715, states,

'Stalbridge is a market town in which there has been a
Paedobaptist congregation ever since the Revolution.'

Further evidence is gathered from the Stalbridge Parish Register, where it is recorded that in 1696, a collection for Broughton in Hampshire, (disaster not stated), amounted to 5s.2d. taken in St. Mary's Church, and 6s.4½d. in the Meeting House, which suggests that there was a considerable number of dissenters and that they were more numerous, or perhaps more generous, than the parishioners of St. Mary's.

In the latter part of the seventeenth century, the minister of the Presbyterians was the Rev. John Sprint, who came from Wimborne to Stalbridge, 'where he had the care of a respectable body of people,' but '. . . such was the spirit of his neighbourhood at Stalbridge', that he and his family had to be removed by a special order of the justices to Sturminster. Through his friends' persuasion and the generosity of a 'gentleman of fortune', who leased him a small estate, he remained as minister to Stalbridge until 1700.

John Sprint must have been a noted preacher, for during his time in Stalbridge, two of his sermons were printed. The first one, published in London, he entitled, 'The Christian mourner comforted . . . By John Sprint, the meanest and unworthiest servant of the best and greatest Master. It included 'the funeral practices of the heathens . . . unworthy of a Christian's imitation, and The Lawfulness of Mourning at the Christian Funeral, and In What Cases it is Justifiable.' was preached in October, 1691, in Stalbridge at the funeral of Mrs Susanna Tyte, wife of the late Thomas Tyte, senior.

At a wedding in Sherborne in May 1699, John Sprint boldly stated in his sermon, The Bride-woman's Counsellor, that 'it is the duty incumbent on all married women to be extraordinary careful to content and please their husbands.'

Two ladies, Lady Chudleigh and Miss Singer, were so sorely provoked that they published a printed reply in verse, 'The Ladies' Defence . . . ', in which the parson says of women that he has

> 'Taught them their husbands to obey and please,
> And to their humours sacrifice their ease:
> Give up their reason, and their wills resign,
> And every look and every thought confine.'

Melissa, the spokeswoman, asks on behalf of her sex,

> 'But unto us is there no deference due?'

– some early women's rights campaigners, no doubt, unwilling to make a subservient bow to the traditional male role as head of the household.

Fifteen years later, however, when John Sprint's daughter married Rev. Henry Rutter, who had succeeded her father at Stalbridge, the tone of the sermon entitled, 'The Bride-groom's Counsellor and the Bride's Comforter', was somewhat altered for it began, 'I shall prove that it is the duty of husbands to please their wives.'

It was during the Rev. Henry Rutter's ministry, (the Rev. John Sprint having left for Milborne Port in 1700), that the first chapel for Presbyterians was built in Stalbridge.

In 1712, Peter Walter, Lord of the Manor of Stalbridge, had signed a Lease for a building on the north side of Guggleton Street (now Station Road), to be used as a Meeting House, and a further Lease in 1723, other signatories at the latter date being Henry Rutter, clerk, Wm Tite sen., John Ryall, Samuel Tite, Joseph Tite, Thomas Metyard, Stephen Fezard sen.

In 1724, a new building was in use; the Certificate issued at the Quarter Sessions held in Bridport, 1724, records:

> 'At this Court was brought a Certificate That there is a New Erected House, called the Meeting House, situate in Stalbridge in this County which is designed to be set apart for the Worshipp of God by a Congregation of Dissenting.
>
> Protestants called Presbiterians and desired that the Same might be entred (sic) amongst the Records of this Court. This Court doth thereupon Record the Same, and the Same is hereby recorded.'

The new building was situated in Guggleton Street, (now Station Road), on the site next to the cottages that later became Meader's shop.

Towards the end of his ministry in Stalbridge, the Rev. Henry Rutter was mentioned in the will, dated 25th October, 1725, of John Ryall, button maker, who had but 'lately purchased' Newnhams (now Ryalls) Farm. The annual sum of £5 was to be paid half-yearly to the minister, as long as he should live in Stalbridge 'and preach the gospel there', but only after John Ryall's decease.

It is not likely that he received his bequest because John Ryall did not die until 1735, before the Rev. Henry Rutter left for South Petherton and was replaced by Rev. Samuel Grinstead.

John Ryall's bequests to his wife, who was childless, and to relatives and friends, of land and almost £2,000 in money, suggest that he was one of the more wealthy inhabitants of Stalbridge. From his signature on the Lease of the Meeting House and his Will, he appears to have been a firm supporter of the Presbyterian Church in Stalbridge.

Peter Walter, Lord of the Manor, in 1712. Stephen Fezard, also a Lessee, was one of the witnesses to Ryall's Will in 1725.

It is not surprising therefore, that John Ryall should leave a bequest for a mourning ring, as well as money, to the Presbyterian minister, but there was to be a ring also for the Rev. Richard Wright, Rector of St. Mary's Church and one for the schoolmaster, Alexander Dyer.

As long as the schoolmaster should teach in Stalbridge, he was to be paid £2 annually for instructing 4 boys, 2 from Henstridge and 2 from Stalbridge in reading, writing and arithmetic.

Jonathon (sic) Ryall, John's brother was to be given one suit of his best 'woolen and linnen', his nephew was to receive his next best suit of 'woolen and linnen', and 'the worst of his woolen and linnen' was to be divided equally between Jonathon Sansome and John Coott of Henstridge.

From a religious census taken in Stalbridge by the Rev. William Lowe, Rector of St. Mary's Church, it is possible to learn the total number of Dissenters in the parish during the final year of the Rev. Samuel Grinstead's ministry. The census was taken in 1738 by 'Mr Curry', probably the Edward Curray, Schoolmaster, who in the same year produced a map of Stalbridge.

Out of a total of 1257 inhabitants, 177 were Dissenters, there being 128 in the Town, 9 in Weston, 39 in Thornhill, and 1 in Gummershay.

This number constitutes a large proportion of Dissenters, with a long tradition in Stalbridge, which makes it surprising that not thirty years later, Wesley was experiencing troublesome behaviour in his visits to Stalbridge, which only ended after a law suit against some of the inhabitants.

Following the Rev. Samuel Grinstead to the Stalbridge ministry, the Rev. Mr Herbert, a Welshman, 'a good scholar, fine in person and of gentlemanly manners',preached Arian sentiments, but gave a period of stability by staying twelve years.

The next minister, Rev. John Hellier, died of consumption in 1754 after a short residence of only two or three years, and for some time

'the church . . . was without the advantage of pastoral care, and declined in spirituality and a regard to vital godliness.'

Some would place the blame on Arianism, (the doctrine that Christ is not consubstantial with God), but it was during the next decade that the followers of John Wesley became the butt of a section of Stalbridge intolerance, which resulted in the lawsuit aforementioned.

For four years, another Welshman of Arian sentiments, the Rev. Moses Davis, ministered to the Stalbridge Presbyterians, John Gray, a respectable farmer in the area, exerted his influence and enjoyed the satisfaction of seeing his son, the Rev. William Gray, a man of 'unbounded enthusiasm and unwearied zeal', established as Minister in 1761. William Gray encouraged his congregations for as long as fifty-three years.

Of Mr Gray, it was written that

' . . . his evangelical sentiments and holy conversation were made eminently useful to the church in inordinating the errors which had crept in.'

Mr Gray died in 1814, having achieved 'a total revolution of religious sentiment', in Stalbridge.

The names of the Trustees of Stalbridge Congregational Church in 1788 are to be found on an Assignment of Bond and leasehold of one acre of land, Westwood, in Corfe Castle. The names given are Joseph Tite, Hosier, Richard Strong, Maltster, R.Grimsteed, Apothecary, and Charles Green Apothecary.

Among the supporters of the church were Richard Strong, who bequeathed money in his Will to the Dissenting Ministers in 1815, and likewise Jonathan Grey, whose Will was dated 1825.

After the long stability of Mr Gray's ministry, which ended when he died in 1814, there followed a period of changes for Stalbridge and Templecombe with students from Western College fitting in between the Rev. Theophilus Eastman and Rev. John Horsey, who left in 1822/3.

During the next ten years, the congregations of Stalbridge and Henstridge, united in 1821, heard the preachings of the Rev. Mr. Simper, Rev. Mr. Kent, Rev. J. Berry and Mr. Sparks.

The latter only stayed six months, having to leave due to pecuniary embarrassments in which he was involved previous to his settlement in Stalbridge, but during his stay, the Chapel at Stalbridge underwent considerable alterations.

In retrospect, it seems remarkable that a new place of worship should be built only two to three years later, after the arrival of the Rev. Antonio Bisenti.

The reason, however, was the necessity due to increased numbers, and the building was erected on a piece of freehold land at a cost of £600, and opened on 23rd September, 1834, by the Rev. Wm. Jay of Bath, Tho Evans of Shaftesbury and Richard Keynes of Blandford.

A licence for the solemnization of marriages was granted to the Chapel, then known as the Independent, during the same year.

In 1832, the Rev. A. Bisenti of Horningsham had been invited to come to Stalbridge for three months, when the salary was £80 per annum, but his term of office lasted for 35 years.

The sum of £200 was raised by the united congregations and the debt for Chapel building was cleared by 1839.

Of the congregation at this time, there is a record of Elias Harding going to Australia in 1833, and C.G. Lush transferring to the Independent Chapel in Newfoundland in 1836: the Minister's daughter Lemira, married Richard Lydford, Teacher of Music in Stalbridge.

The widow of Rev. Antonio Bisenti married the organist of St.Mary's, a much younger man, who is reputedly to have married the lady for her money. There is a report of his even more scandalous behaviour, that he tried to pull out his wife's tongue to murder her, but failed.

He did, however, have to leave his position as church organist and there is a record of him having to leave Stalbridge after this dreadful affair.

According to the Tithe Map of 1838, the Presbyterian Meeting House was situated alongside Guggleton Street on the the same site as the Pump House.

Not far from the Pump House stands an old building, now incorporated into Meader's buildings, which is also shown on the Tithe Map and which, by tradition, has been known as the old Chapel. The plot can be identified as the one which stood next to the Cottages which became Meader's shop, on which in 1885 the Pump House was built.

The Chapel, known as the Independent during the early nineteenth century, registered for the solemnization of marriages in 1834, was in use until the building of the present large Congregational Church, which was built for rapidly expanding Victorian populations on the south side of Station Road, (formerly Guggleton Street), in 1870.

METHODISM IN STALBRIDGE

The middle of the eighteenth century saw disturbances, resulting in a court case, of a different kind from that in the seventeenth century, which had taken place when the inhabitants rose against the Lord of the Manor, Lord Audley for enclosing the Old Park.

Yet these disturbances were taking place just at the time of the enclosure of the New Park by Edward Walter in 1760: this enclosure seems to have provoked no opposition.

During the years preceding 1766, some members of the Stalbridge community had shown religious intolerance by assaulting persons and damaging the property of the followers of Wesley. This resulted in the rioters finally being taken before the Court of the King's Bench for persecuting the Methodists.

Wesley himself wrote in his journal of the length of time it had taken to find justice. He arrived in Stalbridge on Saturday, 30th August 1766.

'Sat. 30 We rode to Stalbridge, long the seat of war, by a senseless, insolent mob, encouraged by their betters, so called, to outrage their neighbours. For what – why, they were mad; they were Methodists. So, to bring them to their senses, they would beat their brains out. . . They broke their windows, leaving not one whole pane of glass, spoiled their goods, and assaulted their persons with dirt and rotten eggs and stones whenever they appeared in the street. But no magistrate, though they appealed to several, would shew them either mercy or justice. At length they wrot to me. I ordered a lawyer to write to the rioters. He did so, but they set him at nought. We then moved the Court of King's Bench. By various artifices they got the trial put off from one assizes to another for eighteen months. But it fell so much the heavier on themselves when they were found guilty; and from that time, finding there is law for Methodists, they have suffered them in peace. I preached near the main street, without the least disturbance, to a large and attentive congregation.'

Wesley returned again to Stalbridge on his mission across Dorset two years later, when, on 28th September 1768, at 1p.m. he preached in Stalbridge 'to a large and seriously attentive congregation,' before going on to 'cold uncomfortable Shaftesbury' where he spoke 'exceeding strong words.'

On Wesley's recommendation, the early followers were encouraged to attend morning worship in their parish church and then meet in one of their member's homes. In Stalbridge the kitchen of Mr and Mrs Hawke was used for services.

John and Mary Hawke were two of the Methodists converted by Wesley, in whose large kitchen, Wesley 'was accustomed to preach.' It was written of Mrs Hawke that she was highly esteemed by Wesley and on several occasions she accompanied him in his carriage when preaching in the neighbourhood.

Peter Hawke, son of John and Mary, was born in Stalbridge, on 21st July 1783, and baptized in the parish church on 2nd August. He left Stalbridge in 1801 to become a writing master in Wimborne Grammar School, later becoming the proprietor of a private school. He became a prominent Methodist leader in Wimborne, where there was also initial opposition to Methodism, but gained a reputation as a pious and esteemed figure, bereaved by many when he died in 1867.

Leases in the Stalbridge Estate Survey of 1811 show that a dwelling and land on the life of Peter Hawke were situated in the Old Swan Yard, when the Swan had been on the west side of the High Street; perhaps this is the old home which accommodated Wesley when he preached in the kitchen.

The first Wesleyan Chapel was opened in 1833, at a cost of £170 with sittings for 200 people, and belonged to the Sherborne Circuit. Stalbridge was only the second place in the Sherborne Circuit to have its own Chapel, the first being Holwell in 1827.

The building was situated on the north side of Guggleton Street, not far from the Congregational Chapel, then known as the Independent.

The remains of this building are now buried under the floor of Williams shop in Station Road, (once Guggleton Street).

A few years ago, before the new shop was erected, it was possible to see the markings where the pews had been, and to imagine the fervour that surrounded the building of that first Wesleyan Chapel.

The much larger Chapel was built in 1873 in Ring Street, after the laying of the Memorial Stone on 1st May. The opening ceremony was on 15th October.

Since Methodist Union in 1932, by Act of Parliament, the Wesleyan Chapel became known the Stalbridge Methodist Church.

TWENTY

The Georgian Town

TRADES & OCCUPATIONS

A picture of life in Stalbridge in the eighteenth century has been made possible by bringing together material and items from many different sources, from Parish Registers, Wills, Indentures and other documents.

Some occupations of the Stalbridge residents, which were entered until 1708/9, can be gleaned from the earliest available parish register begun in 1691. They give some indication of the types of work done by the Stalbridge inhabitants:-

> husbandsman; servant; labourer; shoemaker; hatter; comber; weaver, mercer; taylor; smith; miller; glover; soap boyler; yeoman; victualler; innkeeper; maltster; baker; button maker.

The list of occupations suggests a community providing for its own inner needs, with butcher, baker, miller, maltster, victualler, processing local crops and produce.

Yeoman, husbandsmen, and labourers denote the agricultural workers. Some men were designated as 'poor', which suggests lack of full-time employment or the sick, disabled and old.

More material needs were met by the 'soapboyler', smith, shoemaker, hatter, glover, tailor, and barber who was also the chyrurgeon.

Evidence of trades that possibly depended on economic connections outside Stalbridge can be seen in the occupations weaver, woolstead comber, mercer and button maker. Early indication of Stalbridge's connection with the hosiery trade, later described by Defoe, is given in a Lease of 1668 to Robert Tyte, worsted hosier. One hundred years later, in 1768, another indenture describes several members of the Tite family as hosiers.

A further list of persons and occupations, taken from Dorset Depositions in the first half of the eighteenth century is given at the end of this chapter.

SURVEY OF THE MANOR 1705

By the year 1705, Stalbridge Manor and estate belonged to Peter Walter, former Steward of Richard Newman of Fifehead Magdalen, who owned an estate and lands in the parish of Stalbridge and had claimed being over-rated for the Poor Rates in 1693/4.

The surveys carried out for Peter Walter are invaluable for the information given before the years of the Census Returns, and, from these and other documents surviving, it is possible to derive some details about life in Stalbridge during the eighteenth century. For eighty years, Stalbridge affairs were linked with the Walter family as Lords of the Manor.

In 1705, Peter Walter ordered William Drew, Churchwarden, to provide information for a Survey which gave the names of all the 146 tenants of dwellings and closes on the 1724 acres of his Stalbridge Estate.

The number of tenants in the Survey holding dwellings and closes of land on 1724 acres was 146, and the detailed rental enables us to see which land was tenanted, with the field names and acreage leased or rented to each tenant.

The number of tenants cultivating the land, on the strip system because of the sharing of fields or closes, was 85, with acreage from 1 to 109 acres. Only 9 tenants held more than 50 acres of land under the tenancy of Peter Walter. There is, unfortunately, no other documentation to compare how many acres were held by the freeholders of Stalbridge, nor maps of the holdings.

It is a most revealing document about early eighteenth century Stalbridge showing the placement of tenants and dwellings and also the names of fields under cultivation and pasturage; it reveals that many tenants relied upon the fruits of their labours in agriculture, even though some may have had other occupations.

The details of houses where street names are given unfortunately cannot be related to names and occupations from the Parish Register as so many names are duplicated, not only from father to son, but also from family to family relationship.

However, the number of houses on the Rental, even though an unknown fraction of the whole of Stalbridge dwellings, reveals the expanding town of Stalbridge along Back Lane, Ring Street and Guggleton and the Common.

A list of Stalbridge Tenants in 1705 is given below; many surnames will be familiar today and although exact placings of most houses is impossible, there are some who may pick out former occupants of their dwellings. It will be noticed that some tenants held leases of more than one house.

(Twenty one houses were unplaced in the Survey and it is not known how many other dwellings were privately owned.)

1705 STALBRIDGE TENANTS

MIDDLE of the TOWN
John Joy, Dorothy Locke, Lewis Morgan holds an Inn called the Hinde with Outhouses and Garden, Jonas Pavett, George Pooll, (Swan Yard), Robert Rogers, George Tyte, Robert Tyte of Church Hill, Thomas Tyte of Horsepond, Thomas Tyte of Broad Stone, Thomas Wilmott.
Lewis Morgan of The Hinde paid £10, the rest paid from £2 to £6 rent. John Willoughby holds the Inn called the Black Lyon & the Tolls of the Fairs & Marketts (£10 rent). The Black Lyon Inn was on the south side of Gold Street at its junction with High Street.
Gartrude Gartrell holds a Messuage Garden Backside in the great Street lately the Swan.

PARSONAGE
Near the Parsonage – Abraham Townsend, Christian Ware, Nicholas Watts.
Over against the Parsonage – Robert Gibbons.

GOULD STREET
Thomas Coombe, William Duffet, Jane Foot, Elizabeth Green, Thom/s Hunt,
William Hunt, Mary Murray, Elizabeth Rookcliffe Dec'd, Hannah Snooke,
Willm Snooke, Jonathan Snooke, James Tyte, Mary Young, Dorothy Young.
Rent £1 to £7

GUGGLETON STREET & LANE
William Browne (2 houses), Thomas Murray (3 houses), John Dyke,
Richard Parsons (Stanbrook), Richard Snooke, Joseph Simms,
Martha Simms, James Snookes, Thomas Tyte of Broadstone, William Tyte.
Rents paid were from £1 to £6.

BARROW HILL
Charles Chaunt, Phillipp Chaffey, John Grimes, Thomas Turk, George Tyte.
Thomas Drew near Barsell Bridge.

BACK LANE
Widow Duffett, John Doler, Widow King, Richard Lymmon, Edward Oliver,
Benjamin Randall, William Rideout, Christoph/r Snooke, John Tyte, Widow
Duffett.
Rents £1 to £4.

CHURCH HILL
Elizabeth Burke, William Drew, John Galley, William Harris, Robert Tyte,
Robert Gerrard, John Chamberlain (near the Church).
Edward Bapstocke near the Warren Wall; William Chamberlaine near the
Wood;
Sarah Day near Green Lane; Josias Langdon under the Mannor Wall.
Rents from £1 to £4.

DREW'S LANE
William Drew

THE RING
Edith Bastable, William Browne, Christopher Browne, William Hayne
Sarahg Hayne. Joane Lockett, John Lymmon, William Mullett, Jane Rogers,
Henry Watkins.
Rents £1.10s to £6.

STALBRIDGE COMMON
Henry Allen near the Lodge House, John Browne near Kings Mill Lane,
Thomas Cole near Wilcox Bridge, Dorothy Davies, Hugh Ellis near the Lodge,
William Hunt near Larkwood, Edith Jeanes – a place called the Bow, Henry

Jeanes near the Cottage last mentioned, Richard Lymmon near Wilcox Bridge, Widow Lymmon, Frances Mullins near Wilcox Bridge, Lawrence Pooll near Wilcox Bridge, John Roll, Richard Sharpe, James Seniour, Willm Sherring, Anne Snooke.
Rents £1 to £3.10s.

CAULE (CALE) BRIDGE
James Seniour.

Hill LANE
John Burge DOLLIVERS HAMM – Joane Young

BIBORNE (BIBBERNE) LANE
Mary Dyke

SURVEY OF THE MANOR 1719

A further Survey of the Manor of Stalbridge was completed for Peter Walter in 1719, and there is a special entry for the 'Manor House, Garden, Orchard, Court Yard and Park,' which occupied 50 acres.

The number of tenants in Stalbridge in 1719 had increased to 160, renting 1834 acres. Three tenants rented premises which had licences, namely The Black Lyon, The Swan and The Hind, although later in the century, several other persons were granted licenses.

It is interesting to see that Gold Street is written in the earlier Survey as Gould Street, perhaps an indication of its origin, although the later survey shows alternate spellings, as with the words 'Common' and 'Comon', suggesting the uncertain hand of the writer.

From the large numbers of people included in the Surveys of 1705 and 1719 renting quantities of land over one acre, it is certain that much time was spent by the tenants in the cultivation of their strips of land, which provided them with a living if sufficient, and an income if there was surplus. Possibly some, who could employ more labour, had two occupations.

LIFE IN STALBRIDGE

A Charity School was set up in Stalbridge in 1708 'for teaching some of the poor Boys to read, write and cast Accompt, at the Charge of the Minister of the Place'.

From Defoe's visit to 'Stourbridge, vulgarly call'd Strabridge' in the 1720's, there must have been a considerable number of people employed in the manufacture of stockings. The hand knitting-trade for fine stockings, for which the town and country round had once been famous for making the 'finest, best, and highest priz'd stockings in England', had unfortunately suffered and become 'much decayed' by the increase of the knitting-stocking engine or frame.

During the early part of the century, whilst some villagers were showing religious fervour and swelling the congregation of the Dissenters granted a Lease on the Meeting House in Guggleton Street in 1712, others were demonstrating their views in more temporal ways. By virtue of a mandate received from the Bishop of the Diocese of Bristol in 1729, Hugh Coxhead was denounced to be excommunicated 'during divine service after the Nicene creed.'

Just one year later in Sept 1730, thirteen inhabitants of Stalbridge signed a petition to the Justices of the Peace requesting the removal of a license because

'Mary Meetyard, widow of the parish, keepeth a very disorderly House in selling the Beer, Cider and Brandy on Sunday and other unreasonable times, and has made several people drunk therewith to the great Hurt and Nuisance of her Neighbours.'

Needless to say, the Alehouse was 'put down'.

ALEHOUSE LICENCES

The Alehouse licences granted to Stalbridge in the eighteenth century between 1714 and 1770 give some indication of the number of establishments selling ale and cider, licences being granted to persons until 1753; it is only possible to name the licensed premises until 1770, after which date, documentation is not available, but by collating information from Rentals and other sources, it has been possible to link some names with premises before 1753.

In 1714, William Drew held one licence and Christopher Snooke and Edward Curry two each. From the Rental Book, William Drew lived on Church Hill, where, according to a later lease, there was an Inn called the Rose and Crown.

Following the five licences granted in 1714, the number rose to nine in 1718, reaching a maximum of fifteen in 1753; only three Inns were named in the Stalbridge Rentals of the Lord of the Manor, 1705 to 1749, these being The Hind, The Black Lyon and The Swan.

Of the licensees in 1718, it seems certain that Joshua Poole, who held a licence for over twenty years, owned or managed The Ship; his family held it until at least 1770.

Other licensees in 1718 were Edward Curry, William Drew, Philip Senior, Sara Hayne, John Payne, Edward Hellyer (who lived in Back Lane), Martin Lemon, and Thomas Tite, Junior.

Licences appeared to lapse occasionally, Christopher Snooke (two licences in 1714) renting the premises, late The Swan in 1719, yet being granted one licence again in 1720.

The selling of ale must have become a profitable means of making a living, keeping the brewers also fully occupied if one looks at the rate of increase in licences, from five in 1714, twelve in 1720, thirteen in 1736, eleven in 1746, and a maximum of sixteen in 1753.

The names of persons granted licences in 1753 were William Galpin (Red Lion), John Dowding (The Swan), Mary Senior (The Hoop), William Tite

(The George), Matthew Allwood (lived on the Common near the Puxey, also gamekeeper to Peter Walter, – The Buffalo's Head), Thomas Jeanes (no sign), Thomas Hussey (no sign), John Grimes (The Parrot), Joan Edwards (Hare & Hounds), John Lemmon (Black Lyon), John West (White Hart), Edward Weare (The Hind), Joseph Harris (Rose & Crown), Susannah Strong (no sign), Charles Parsons, Robert Lindfields (The Ship).

The year, 1755, saw a significant drop in licensees in Stalbridge, when the number was reduced to seven.

For reasons, one might consider the effects of a recommendation from the 1752 meeting of the Dorset Quarter Sessions, which Court, taking into consideration the

'great increase of common Alehouses or Victualling houses' . . . 'after many complaints made against loose or disorderly Alehouses and which are by this Court deemed one great Cause for the increase of Vagrants and other idle and disorderly persons, they being much encouraged by such alehouses, . . . to prevent . . . abuses for the future doth recommend no licence no licence be granted without certificate from the parish authority.'

Another pointer to the drop in licences may have been the presence in 1753 of Thomas Gill of Stalbridge, who was one of His Majesty's Gauges for the duty of Excise on Beer, Ale, etc. and in order to be deemed fit for the work, it had been necessary for him to appear at the meeting of the Dorset Quarter Sessions

'and then and there in open Court between the hours of nine and twelve in the forenoon upon the oaths of two credible witnesses did make it appear that he had received the Sacrament of the Lord's Supper according to the Usuage of the Church of England and thereupon did then and there take the Oaths of Allegiance Supremacy and Abjuration and Subscribe the Declaration against Transubstantiation according to the Several Acts of Parliament in that case made and provided.'

There is no record of how well he did his duty, but his presence may have somewhat reduced the trade in substandard beer and ale.

From 1756, the reduced number of establishments granted licences in Stalbridge and their licensees were The Red Lion (William Galpin), who kept the Inn until he died in Sep, 1778, Swan (John Dowding), Black Lyon (Susannah Strong), White Hart (John Lemmon), Hind (Edmund Weare), Hare and Hounds (Charles Parsons), Ship (Joseph Poole).

From 1763, The Fowler was licensed by William Parsons, when the Hare and Hounds ceased trading, it continued to be held by one William Parsons, carpenter, in 1811 on a lease dating from 1770; from 1763 The Shovel was run by Charles Parsons, who ceased trading there in 1769, to take over The Hind, unlicensed from 1764 to 1770.

The siting of some of the Inns, using tithe map references and earlier surveys with different reference numbers, rentals and lease details, has not been easy and confusion arises from some lease entries, overwritten by later clerks.

It is known from the Rental Books that the Hind was split into two separate establishments for part of the eighteenth century, but it is not certain that the north part was The Hind, and the south part The White Hart, The Swan in 1784 being on the west side of the High Street (part of Silk Hays). In 1811, however, The Swan was situated next to The Hind, the plot on the west side of the High Street being designated as the 'late Swan Inn' in the Survey of that year for Lord Uxbridge.

The licensee of the Black Lyon also paid Poor Rate on the Tolls of the Market. Being situated on the corner of the south side of Gold Street and the High Street, opposite the Cross, the owner was in a fair position for the taking of tolls and charges for standings and baskets at the market, no doubt held around the Cross.

According to Lady Theodora Grosvenor writing in the 1870s, the site of the Ship Inn was opposite the gate leading to Ryall's Farm, on the Bagber Road south of Stalbridge. It was evidently 'a famous centre in the neighbourhood for such diversions as bull-baiting and cock-fighting, which were also in vogue on Marnhull Common within the memory of persons now living'. (1873)

She also wrote

' . . . on the halter-path to Sturminster Newton, stood till very recently, a small cottage, consisting of about two rooms, which as known by the imposing name of the Golden Gate, in which the Magistrates' meetings of the division were held. In the wall, just above the door, in the gable end of the house, was a stone with a gate of four bars cut on it, with the letters R.J.M. over it, and the date, 1748, below it. The gate was always kept brightly gilt, and the stone is now carefully preserved at Barrow Hill, at Stalbridge.

No legend remains which can explain the origin of the Golden Gate, but it was a curious and out-of-the -way place for the local magistrates to meet in.'

Golden Gate was the birthplace of William Barnes, the Dorset poet, whose family soon afterwards went to live at Rushay in Bagber.

STALBRIDGE LANDMARKS

A new landmark had been erected at Thornhill in 1727 in the form of an obelisk to mark the accession of George II by Sir James Thornhill, who by his presence and interest in restoring his ancestor's estates, must have induced a new impetus (and perhaps employment) into the area.

Curray's map of 1738 shows the main routes through Stalbridge and the tracks used by travellers around the small market town, many of whom must have travelled on foot from the surrounding areas, especially on market days and during the period of the two fairs in Stalbridge in May and September.

Some of these traditional lines of communications were lost after the mid-eighteenth century when Edward Walter, made the most dramatic change by enlarging Stalbridge Park. This involved enclosing certain highways and land leased to tenants and cutting off some of the long established routes to Sherborne and Henstridge.

It also added another feature to Stalbridge, a five mile length of wall around the new park of almost 500 acres, ten times in size of the old park, which no doubt gave much extra work to the local quarries and masons.

By the enclosure of Stalbridge Park, the following lanes radiating from the Old Park sank into antiquity; these were Green Lane, Sherborne Road, Ruthorne Lane, Midddleway Lane, Furge Lane, and Horseward Lane.

From Peter Walter's Rental of 1749, we know that there were at least 156 houses at that time, undoubtedly the number was greater than this because it is not likely that all the houses belonged to the estate.

The closest estimate of population by the mid-eighteenth century must be assumed from the census taken by the Rector of Stalbridge in 1738, who was interested in the number of Dissidents in the parish. The number of inhabitants was then given as 1257.

OVERSEERS' ACCOUNTS

The first Account Book began in 1756 when there were 34 poor recipients receiving £9.16s.

This number rose to 48 in May 1775, reducing to 41 in June 1782, rising again to 48 in 1794. The number of those receiving money payments fell dramatically after this to 30 in June, 1799, but it seems likely that the Bastardy Lists were kept separate from this time, although records are incomplete to verify, but there were 46 on the Bastardy List in 1801 and 52 in 1805.

Some examples of relief for the poor of Stalbridge, apart from the money payments, can be seen in the following items allowed in 1758.

1758		
May To John Jeans for thatching at the Silk House	4s 10d
a Gown and Petticoat for Rose Snook	12s 6¼d
½ A Thousand of Nails for ye Silk House	1s 3d
Sarah Sims for Clark's bastard	5s 0d
Jude Brown for Clark's bastard	3s 0d
A Shirt for Allwoods Boy	1s 8d
Cloth for Bucks Boy	16s 6d
A Shift for Mary Buck	3s 0d
Geo Pools wife sick	1s 0d
Henry Mullens lame	2s 0d
Wm Lambert a Bill for Shoes	12s 3d
To the Doct at Curing Clarks Dauger	8s 0d
June 11 Ed Brown for destroying Rats at W/house	7s 6d
New Book for Accts	4s 6d
July 9 A pr of Hose for Saml Senior's Maidd	8d
A coffin for Wm Cricket's wife	7s 0d

Wm Lambert's Bill for Shoes	12s 4d
Aug 6 Mary Lemon Maid Shroud Coffin Bell to grave	11s 8d
Thos Lemon's Boy Shroud Coffin Bell to grave	11s 8d
Tho Browne Girdle 2 Shifts 1pr Hose	4s 4d
Sep 3 Jos Randell 6 Girdles for ye Itch	6s 0d
Jos Randell for ointment	1s 0d
Wm Grimsteed's Bill (Doctor)	£3 3s 7d
Oct 1 A Red Tie for Grace Peans & making	4s 6d
1759	
Mar For Clothing four Boys in Order for the Sea Service	£ 6 1s 1d
A pr of breeches for Crudy Ellis	4s 7d
Taylor's Bill for above cloth	£1 3s 3d
A pr of hose for Grace Peans	1s 1d
1759 Apr Bill for repairing Thatch at the W/house	4s 9½d

It was, of course, incumbent upon the Overseers to set a Poor Rate and collect it, charges being made upon certain properties and pieces of land, copses, woods, and even the Tolls of the Market and the Fairs collected by the Black Lyon.

In addition to the Poor Rate, the Overseers collected from the men involved in paternity suits, for the lying in and weekly upkeep of children, and they also received £3.3s.0d rent for the Silk House from Mr Ward (1782) when the total monies collected were £501.4s.4d and the amount disbursed £479.16s.8¾d

A more profitable gain was to be had when substitutes were provided for men ballotted for the Militia; one example in 1782 is of Mr Lambert, Dorchester, paying the Overseers the highest sum of £9.12s.0d. for Sam Biss to take his place.

During 1782/3 jackets sold to the poor amounted to £2.16s.6d. At 1d per jacket this was a tremendous number, but one wonders how they were made and of what material?

STALBRIDGE RIOTERS

It was reported by the *Western Flying Post* in 1765 that in the spring of that year

'rioters destroyed a bunting mill at Stalbridge, but were driven out of the Market by wool-combers, and attacked a mill at Marnhull. Here the crowd was repulsed by "sixteen stout young fellows of the parish, famous for good back sword players", ... many broken heads and bruised limbs.'

Nothing further has become available by way of explanation; but the following year saw the mob in Stalbridge swelling against Wesley and the Methodists which story is dealt with in the chapter on Dissenters.

SILK TRADE

Silkhouse Barton, just off the High Street, gives evidence of the silk industry in

Stalbridge and a workhouse, burnt down in 1759, and rebuilt at the expense of the parish, was let until 1786, and possibly later, as a silk manufactory at 3gns per year.

The silk trade employed many workers, including the poor in the Workhouses. It appears that there were two, one in Silk House Barton and one at the Ring. In 1770, agreement was reached between the Parish of Stalbridge and Mr Willmott, Silk Man of Sherborne, to

'rise the W/house Childring 6d per wk above what they now have and to rise the two Silk House at the Usual Time as at Other Places in Proportion . . . '

In 1774 Willmott of Sherborne Silk Mills offered to buy Ward's machinery at Stalbridge and to pay the rent there, as he wanted more winding engines.

In 1774, it had been agreed by Vestry

'to lett Mr Warde have the Lower Poore House, to be made a Work House for his Use of Working Silk at the Price of 3 Pounds and 3 shilling a Year . . . '

provided he kept the poor in work.

The Parish also agreed to take down the partitions of the chambers of the house of Mr Richard Fezard without any cost to Mr Willmott, which Mr Fezard was to replace at his own cost when Mr Willmott's time was out.

The agreement suggests that there was work for the poor at that time as the children were being given a rise, but the proviso looked for fluctuations of trade in its request that work be given to Stalbridge poor as long as Mr Ward keep any people at work 'except Bruten'.

The silk supply was to peter out during the Napoleonic War, but Claridge's report stated that in 1793 there were 150 silk workers in Stalbridge, mainly women and children.

The industry must have gradually died out, but the occupation of silk weaver is given in the Parish Register as late as 1829, and pauper silk workers in the Census Returns of 1841.

Of the type of silk work and the product, it is difficult to state, but Stalbridge was always a silk-working area subsidiary to that of Sherborne Silk Mills. It is likely however, that the two 'Silk Men' installed some machinery in Stalbridge. Local tales that silk was grown on mulberry bushes in Stalbridge were hardly likely to be true because of the quantities of silk involved to keep well over 100 workers in employment.

STALBRIDGE TOWN

In R. & J. Dodsley's book on Dorsetshire, published 1764, Stalbridge is dismissed as 'a small inconsiderable place having little worthy of note except its Charity School', only slightly better perhaps than its neighbour, Sturminster Newton, which is described as 'a mean obscure place.'

A late eighteenth century description of Stalbridge stated,

'. . . Here is a good show of cattle every Monday fortnight, it being situated in a very good grazing country . . . and is remarkable for a manufacture of stockings. Great quantities of stone are dug near it',

and of Sturminster Newton, five miles away,

'It is computed that from this place, and within six miles hereof, ten tons of butter are weekly carried to Poole, (exclusive of what is consumed at home) in order to be shipped for Portsmouth and the London markets.'

From the above description, it would appear that Stalbridge could not only have been self-sufficient in dairy products but was also sending away its surplus butter, and presumably had a thriving produce market. There is further evidence of 'grazing produce' being sent to Poole in 1837.

The cattle market had been revived after the American War and Stalbridge was in an advantageous position in North Dorset, there being no other cattle market between Salisbury and Yeovil. The decline of the cattle market in the nineteenth century because of the opposition of the Rector of Stalbridge to the fact that the cattle were lined up to be sold throughout Stalbridge's long street is dealt with in the book, *The Stalbridge Inheritance, 1780-1854*.

NAPOLEONIC WAR

The end of the eighteenth century saw the outbreak of war with France which affected Stalbridge indirectly with its extra taxes, tariffs, and shortage of silk supplies.

Whilst preparations for an invasion by the French of the Dorset coastal areas caused surveys to be made of supplies that could be requisitioned and sent with stock farther inland for safety, Stalbridge, well away from the coastal belt was well out of immediate danger.

No doubt, naughty Stalbridge infants were threatened with the Bogey Man, the common nick-name for Napoleon, but the war must have seemed remote until the drawing up of the Militia Lists in 1799.

Men were drawn from all four tithings, the occupations of nearly all the nineteen recruits in Gomershay, Thornhill and Weston reflecting on the agricultural nature of their work.

From the Stalbridge Town Tithing, men in trade like the innkeeper, the baker, butcher, carpenter, cordwainer, woolcomber, tiler, tailor, and mason did their training alongside the yeomen, labourers, and the two gentlemen, Robert James, Agent to the Lord of the Manor, and Robert Bastin.

These men were between 18 and 45 years of age, some of them married men with children.

Signal stations were set up along the high points and ridges in Dorset, and Stalbridge had the satisfaction of knowing that it would receive warnings of any invasion from the Woolland station on the slopes of Bulbarrow.

In 1796, Lord Henry-William Paget, the eldest son of Earl Uxbridge, who owned Stalbridge House and most of Stalbridge, spent nine weeks in Weymouth with his cavalry regiment. His bills for bread, meat, and other necessities such as candles and charcoal reveal the stylish mode of living. The quantities of wine and spirits must have been consumed very liberally; port was £1.14s. per dozen bottles, sherry £1.18s. Five shillings bought a bottle of brandy or the servant's lodging for a week.

During the same year, this young married man, became Member of Parliament for Milborne Port, a seat which he held until 1810. His father, the Earl of Uxbridge was appointed Deputy Lieutenant for Dorset.

It was not until nearly twenty years later that the young Cavalry officer was to become a national hero at the Battle of Waterloo and to leave behind a legacy to Stalbridge in the shape of the Anglesey Cottages.

SIZE OF STALBRIDGE IN 1801

The Census Returns of 1801 cover the four tithings of Stalbridge Town, Gomershay, Thornhill and Weston. There were 251 houses containing 251 families with 551 males and 694 females, making a total of 1245 persons, a number slightly less than the total of 1257 taken in the 1738 Survey by the Rector of Stalbridge.

A list of Depositions and disputes from the eighteenth century is given here because it reveals names and somewhat varied occupations of some Stalbridge inhabitants before the official Census Return of 1801.

Depositions taken at the house of Edith West, being a public house in Stalbridge 14 Dec 1741. Bower v Banger.

Plaintiff Frances Bower & wife, Catherine, widow of Abraham Townsend, Jane Drake, Mary Burge, John Dowding and Samuel Hanny.

Defendants Samuel and Mary Banger, and Samuel Cave.

Re- estate of Samuel Cave (deceased) of Stalbridge, gent.

States Bond given 11 Jan 1695 by James Cave of Stalbridge Yeoman to James Jennings, Samuel Bowles and William Langdon, then constable and churchwardens of Stalbridge. In 1717 William Drew and Willliam Duffett were Churchwardens of Stalbridge and William Chamberlaine, Lawrence Bracher, Matthew Hunt and John Allard Overseers of the Poor.

Ann Lock, widow of Stalbridge was sister in law of John Tittershill whose Daughter Ann married William Senior and whose daughter Mary married Robert Senior.

Elizabeth Tyte of Stalbridge, spinster, Richard Coombe after 1721 married Susanna Follett of Stalbridge, spinster, 15 Oct 1723, a neice of Eliz Chafe of Stalbridge, Baker. Indenture witness was Alexander Dyer of Stalbridge, writing master, now deceased.

William Rowcliffe married Eliz Tyte c 1723-1729

Jonathan Ryall, executor of John Ryall

Deponents are: –

George Young, yeoman, aged 55

Edward Curray, the younger, writing master, aged 46

Eliz Smith, widow, aged 50

Edward Jeans, thatcher, aged 50

William Pool, labourer, aged 64

John Allard, labourer, aged 50

Thomas Jeans, yeoman, aged 50

Richard Strong, carpenter, aged 44

Samuel Burge, cooper, aged 25

William Rowcliffe, butcher, aged 40

Thomas Combes, gen, aged 75

Henry Mullins, yeoman, aged 70

William Banger, yeoman, aged 44

Mary Watts, spinster, aged 60, daughter of Hepszibah Watts, Widow, who owned land in Stalbridge

Thomas Snooke, carpenter, aged 45

William Senior, husbandman, aged 40, servant to Samuel Cave at £5 a year, with meat, drink, washing & lodging.

Martha Gorman, widow, aged 57, daughter of Robert Gibbon.

James Banger, yeoman, aged 35

Robert Senior, husbandman, aged 48

Stephen Fezard, yeoman, aged 64

Anne Browne, widow, maiden name Coxhill, aged 45

Hercules Plowman, gen, aged 75, Churchwarden in 1720

Phillip Plowman, aged 30, gen, son of above.

Mary Duffett, widow of William Duffett, aged 80

John Bastable, carpenter, aged 59

Mary, wife of John Fezard, butcher, aged 29, daughter of Abraham Townsend, mercer, deceased.

Richard Ellis, husbandman, aged 37.

Following on 24 Dec Castle Inn Sherborne

Richard Coombe, baker, aged 40

– Tite, hosier, aged 45

Matthew Burge, butcher, aged 47

No date Vol X

Richard Downe, Clerk, in Will of Elias Haskett who died in New England

Haskett v Duffett

Wife of William Duffett and his five children also in Will

John & William Calpen, sons of William Calpen, deceased, both under 21

Frances Strong of Stalbridge, widow, aged 36

Selfe v Selfe

A messuage and 30 acres in Stalbridge demised to Abraham Selfe the elder by William Burleton.

George Rabbetts, husbandman.

Postscript

The handover of the Stalbridge Estate from the Walter family to the Pagets of Plas Newydd, Anglesey in 1780 has been fully described in the next in sequence volume of Stalbridge history, *The Stalbridge Inheritance, 1780–1854*, published in 1993.

A few details of leases before 1780 are available but the main rentals and other pieces of information that may have added to our knowledge of life before 1780 have not been retained to give us the sources and amazing small details of life in Stalbridge gained from the mass of the preserved Anglesey documents now in the Dorset Record Office.

Bibliography

MANUSCRIPT SOURCES

British Library
Boyle Papers 40, Samuel Rich petition

Dorset County Record Office
Anglesey Estate Accounts
Dorset Hearth Tax Returns
Dorset Protestation Returns
Dorset Quarter Sessions - Minutes
Stalbridge Church Rate
Stalbridge Churchwarden's Accounts
Stalbridge Overseers Reports
Stalbridge Parish Registers
Sturminster Newton Castle Court Book
Will of Peter Walter
Wills of the Thornhill family

Hertfordshire Record Office
Survey of the Manor of Stalbridge in the County of Dorset belonging to Peter
    Walter Esq, Stalbridge 1705
Survey of the severall tenements & Estates held by Peter Walter Esq
Lord of the Manor of Stalbridge in the county of Dorset 1719

Public Record Office
Sir Robert Boyle's Will
Lismore Papers
Manorial Court Roll Stalbridge Weston 1703
Tax Returns for 1525
Tudor Muster Rolls
Will of Edward Walter 220 1077

Royal Society
Letter 1649 Royal Society

Weymouth Library
The Walpole Papers

BOOKS AND PRINTED SOURCES

Barbey Pollard, W., *Visitation of Dorsetshire* 1565 Exeter, 1887

Bray, W., ed. *Evelyn's Diary*, Warne 1891

Burke's Peerage

Densham & Ogle, *The Congregational Church in Dorset* 1899

Dorset Natural History and Archeological Society Proceedings

Dictionary of National Biography

Fagersten, *Place Names of Dorset*

Finberg, H.P.R., *Early Saxon Charters*

Fry, E.A. *Dorset Feet of Fines*

The Gentleman's Magazine 1832

Grosvenor, Lady Theodora, *Motcombe Past and Present* C.Bastable
    Shaftesbury 1873

Hardy, Thomas, *A Group of Noble Dames*

Hutchins,J., *History of Dorset*

Maddison, R.E.W., *The Life of the Honourable Robert Boyle F.R.S.*, Taylor &
Francis London 1969

Mayo, C.H., *Bibliotheca Dorsetiensis*, Chiswick Press, London 1885

McGarvie, M., *Frome Through the Ages*, Frome Society, 1982

Pope, F.J., *Dorset Depositions*
            Dorset Suits 1696/7

Royal Commission on Historic Monuments

Rich, Mary, *Countess of Warwick*, Journals of Longmans 1901

Simon, J.S., *Methodism in Dorset*, Weymouth 1870

Somerset & Dorset Notes & Queries

Spenser Ashbee, H., *Index of Forbidden Books*, Sphere Books Ltd ,London 1969

Swayne,W.S., *The History and Antiquities of the Town of Stalbridge*

Squibb, G.D., *A Calendar of Dorset Deeds*, Dorset County Record Office

ABBREVIATIONS USED IN TEXT AND SOURCE LISTS

DRO	Dorset County Record Office
DCC	Dorset County Chronicle & Somersetshire Gazette
DCM	Dorset County Museum
DNB	Dictionary of National Biography
HHD	Hutchins J., *The History and Antiquities of the County of Dorset*, Westminster, 3rd Edn 1861-1870
HRO	Hertfordshire Record Office
PRO	Public Record Office
DNH&AS	Dorset Natural History and Archaeological Society
S&D N&Q 1892	Somerset and Dorset Notes and Queries
RCHM	Royal Commission on Historic Monuments
OL	Anglesey, Marquess of, *One Leg*, Cape 1961